ENGAGING WITH HISTORY IN THE CLASSROOM

Grades 6–8

ENGAGING WITH HISTORY IN THE CLASSROOM

The Civil Rights Movement

Janice I. Robbins, Ph.D.,
and Carol L. Tieso, Ph.D.

PRUFROCK PRESS INC.
WACO, TEXAS

Copyright ©2015 Prufrock Press, Inc.

Edited by Lacy Compton

Cover design by Raquel Trevino and layout design by Allegra Denbo

ISBN-13: 978-1-61821-259-7

Prufrock Press Inc.
P.O. Box 8813
Waco, TX 76714-8813
Phone: (800) 998-2208
Fax: (800) 240-0333
http://www.prufrock.com

TABLE OF CONTENTS

ACKNOWLEDGEMENTS

The development of this unit of study required the insight, knowledge, hard work, and support of many people. The expertise and guidance of Dr. Jeremy Stoddard and the willingness of other professors at the College of William and Mary to critique drafts along the way allowed us to move forward with quiet confidence. Supporting contributions were also made by members of three key organizations: the Colonial Williamsburg Foundation and the Street Law and Teaching Tolerance organizations.

Many graduate students worked on initial drafts of unit lessons, including Megan Davidson, Katie Guidry, Sherry Harrell, Meg Hoffman, Ginny Hutcheson, Kristen Kelley, Clifton Lyddane, Catherine Mason, Rebecca Schweitzer, and Sarah Wright.

Effective curriculum is tested and revised. Thanks to participating school districts in Alabama and Virginia, we had the opportunity to gain invaluable feedback related to the implementation of this unit, the effectiveness of lesson activities and assessments, and the perceived impact on students. Special thanks to teachers in Jefferson, Shelby, and Tarrant counties in Alabama; and Fairfax, Norfolk, Prince William, and Williamsburg-James City counties in Virginia.

We are deeply grateful to the staff at Prufrock Press as they patiently lent their expertise as editors, illustrators, and layout designers.

We dedicate this unit to the teachers and students who may find in it sparks that make history come alive as they engage in it within the classroom walls.

UNIT OVERVIEW

INTRODUCTION TO THE ENGAGING WITH HISTORY IN THE CLASSROOM UNITS

Engaging With History in the Classroom is a series of American history units that focus on what it means to be a U.S. citizen, living in a country that expects as much from its citizens as it provides. Learning to be informed, active participants in democracy is the ultimate goal of education and the focus of these units of study.

In each of the four units, middle-grade students develop an understanding of the forces behind the actions and decisions of individuals and groups who struggled to define and acquire the social, economic, and political rights of democratic citizenship.

To facilitate learning that is rich, thoughtful, historically meaningful, and personally engaging, these units have been designed with several ideas in mind. First, the nature of the young adolescent is to be concerned with self and immediate surroundings. Recognizing this, we tried to ensure that the lessons allow for personal connections, peer interaction, and powerful introductions that grab the learner. Second, history is often watered down in the classroom, and taught in a way that leaves the learner passive. To buck this trend, we have made each lesson a path to discovering rather than being told. Students engage in critical reading, thinking, and speaking so that they become original thinkers about what really happened.

Each lesson follows a pattern that guides students from awareness to conceptual understanding, beginning with a motivating introduction and ending with possible extensions for the class or certain members of the class. All lessons are written at a level that expands students' thinking both critically and creatively. Although some readings and discussion activities may be a stretch for some students, with support and, at times, modifications and rehearsal, all students can participate in the same activities at the same time, maintaining their sense of community.

Many of the lessons include small-group work, which allows for instructional decisions about grouping. You might consider offering a lesson extension or a more difficult reading to certain students or offering more scaffolding and support to other students. Small groups should also frequently include mixed-ability learners, offering everyone an opportunity to learn together and from each other.

The Engaging With History in the Classroom units incorporate the following key models and strategies for learning:

➤ concept development;
➤ critical reading, thinking, and reasoning;
➤ discussion and deliberation;
➤ historical perspective recognition;
➤ historical inquiry; and
➤ assessment.

CONCEPT DEVELOPMENT

Two overarching concepts, democratic citizenship and conflict, are central to the Engaging With History in the Classroom units. Specific lessons introduce the concepts and support concept formation. In subsequent lessons, students deepen their understanding through applications that help them access progressively more sophisticated generalizations about each of the concepts. In addition, each unit highlights particular key concepts critical to historical reasoning about the times and events presented.

Additional conceptual development is supported throughout the units, encouraging students to summarize and draw conclusions that support an appropriate storyline for the events being analyzed. Essential questions and statements of conceptual understandings are provided for each lesson in support of the teacher's efforts to help students grow. A discussion of concept development strategies can be found in Appendix A.

CRITICAL READING, THINKING, AND REASONING

In every lesson, students participate in readings followed by key questions that help them focus on ideas and their connections to the sequence of events. Questions are designed at higher levels of thinking and connected to reasoning skills such as understanding point of view, recognizing inferences and assumptions, and using and questioning information. Questions are open-ended, requiring reasoning and encouraging the exploration of an idea. These types of questions allow for a response from every child, not just those who traditionally know the correct answer.

DISCUSSION AND DELIBERATION

Two models of teaching are used to develop student deliberation and discussion skills. The structured academic controversy is a teaching model that requires students to alternately explore and argue for both sides of a controversial issue in order to acquire a balanced opinion on the issue. The Socratic seminar engages students in group dialogue about a common reading. Students examine the text and prepare to respond to open-ended questions that require them to think critically, analyze multiple meanings, and express their ideas with conviction and clarity, using evidence to support their ideas. Both of these models move students from simply debating opposing views to critical analysis and historical synthesis.

HISTORICAL PERSPECTIVE RECOGNITION

Understanding of the past is enhanced through perspective recognition. Learning experiences in the lessons help students make sense of past events, customs, practices, and artifacts in terms of the beliefs, values, resources, environment, and actions of people at the time. Students are asked to put themselves into the shoes of those who experienced the Civil Rights Movement firsthand through readings of primary sources and through role-play experiences.

HISTORICAL INQUIRY

Through planned activities in each unit, students learn to engage in the doing of history. Each lesson begins with a question that is key to that study. The emphasis is on guiding students to ask effective questions, analyze sources, discern what is significant, and defend historical interpretations. At the end of each lesson, students should have grown in conceptual understanding of the issues, the ideas, and the experiences that Americans faced during the Civil Rights Movement. Student activities immerse the learners in seeking thoughtful answers to the key questions.

ASSESSMENT

Each unit of study provides teachers and students with a pre–post assessment design that can be used for formative and summative assessment. In addition, each lesson includes suggestions for summarizing, observing, informally assessing, and student reflections. These can provide both teacher and students with regular feedback on performance. Critical to student learning is the feedback they receive following the presentation of their ideas, whether that presentation is in the form of a traditional quiz or test, their contributions to discussions, their project work, or their responses to key questions posed by the teacher, other students, or themselves. Feedback may be formal or informal, and ways to seek feedback are offered in each lesson. In addition, students are given many opportunities to self-reflect, coming to recognize the patterns of their own learning.

LESSON FORMAT

Lesson at a glance. Each lesson begins with a brief summary of the student activities designed to support the focus question of the lesson. Note that these descriptions are written in terms of student outcomes and may be used as a guide to teaching objectives for both content and process.

Timeline events. Timeline events are provided to situate each lesson within a particular period of time. Teachers and students may use the lesson's events list to add to a class timeline or students' timelines developed throughout the unit. Students often need concrete ways of maintaining a historical perspective on the passage of time within the unit of study. Referring to the timelines and adding comments on key events is one way of guiding students in this critical learning.

Essential questions. In the spirit of inquiry and critical thinking, each lesson includes a set of essential questions that guide the development of understanding essential to the lesson. These questions may be posted at the beginning of each lesson. They may also be used as alternates to the assessment activities suggested in the lesson, as support for summary discussions, and as guides to teaching and checkpoints for the teacher's understanding of the measure of student learning.

Conceptual understandings. The lesson sets of conceptual understandings represent the building blocks that lead to students' understanding of the important ideas of the lesson. Each of these is represented as a statement, not of fact, but of an idea that must be developed by a student through his or her own experiences. Lesson activities guide student thinking so that each of these conceptual understandings becomes part of a student's own framework for the causes and effects of the Civil Rights Movement. When students have deepened their understanding of these important ideas, they are able to make connections, provide details and evidence, and discuss the meaning behind each statement with confidence.

Important terms and ideas. A list of key terms and ideas connected to each lesson is provided. Note that this should not be considered a vocabulary list, but rather a set of ideas that students must be able to conceptualize in order to respond to the unit's essential questions. Terms that are particularly abstract or strange should merit attention in terms of concept development. Others may be familiar to most of the students, but all students should be able to articulate their own understanding of each idea to facilitate use in the unit activities.

Materials. The list of materials includes reproducible handouts provided for the lesson, as well as any classroom supplies that will be needed. Intended as helpful supplements, handouts can be used however you see fit—copied and distributed individually to students, projected for the whole class, or, in some cases, kept by you as an informational teacher resource.

Suggested resources. Trade books, videos, active websites, podcasts, and specific Internet support sites are included in the suggested resources for each lesson. Web addresses were current at the time of publication. Links to these sites can be found at http://www.prufrock.com/Assets/ClientPages/engaging_with_history.aspx

An important part of learning in each unit is the use of technology. Students' guided access to multiple mediums is an important part of the resource component for each lesson. Broadening access to experts in the field, to databases that cannot be replicated at a school site, and to archives rich with primary sources strengthens student learning and offers additional motivation for all students.

A list of suggested historical novels and biographies is provided in Handout 0.1 to encourage students to expand their conceptualization of the lives of people during the Civil Rights Movement. Although most of the suggested books are fiction, they provide reasonably authentic depictions of the era. You are encouraged to select several books for reading groups as part of language arts activities, or offer students the option of developing informal book club groups.

The hook. Hook activities are intended to get all students quickly engaged, so keep this part of the lesson brief. Every lesson offers some hook that may involve a stimulating visual display, a brief role-play, or a participatory activity. Hooks set the stage for the lesson and ensure that the level of student engagement is high from the beginning. You may think of many creative ways to alter the hook for particular lessons, and you are encouraged to do so. Involving a few students in setting up the hook adds to the drama.

Developing conceptual understanding. The heart of the lesson, this is where students are introduced to new ideas, old documents and other forms of evidence, and key questions that enable them to explore possibilities, seek evidence, make judgments, and recognize that even primary sources can present conflicting accounts. Thus, students are asked to think like historians and express their ideas based on reasoning rather than memory.

At times, lesson instructions contain scripted passages for the teacher. Note that these scripts are intended to serve as models for effective lesson implementation, to offer guiding questions, and to assist you, the teacher, in establishing a background for student exploration. The scripts are not necessarily intended to be read word-for-word. Use them as you find them helpful in the flow of the lesson. Your personal, genuine style of presentation is likely to be the most successful. These lessons have been taught in a number of schools prior to publication, and teachers have offered us their best thinking about the sequence of activities as well as the important moves and transitions that seem to work in keeping students engaged and productive.

SOAR: Summarize, observe, assess, reflect. Activities in this part of the lesson enable the teacher and the students to review what new learning has occurred. The teacher will observe the range of achievements, interest, and motivation among individual students and make adaptations as needed. Formal and informal assessments are suggested, and most lessons provide a reflection activity for students.

Think again: Homework. Homework activities are designed as additional opportunities for reflection on the current lesson, to offer teachers a checkpoint for student learning, or to provide extensions of lesson content. In most cases, the homework assignment is not essential to the lesson and can be considered an optional activity. In a few lessons, students are asked to complete an assignment to be used in the next lesson.

Keep on going: Lesson extensions. Because students of different abilities and interests are represented the classroom, lesson extensions are provided to encourage deepened understanding and experience with historical thinking. Extensions should not be reserved for advanced learners alone, but should be made available to all students who are interested in the challenges.

INTRODUCTION TO *ENGAGING WITH HISTORY IN THE CLASSROOM: THE CIVIL RIGHTS MOVEMENT*

Sixty years after the landmark *Brown v. Board of Education* decision of 1954 and its aftermath, United States citizens have much to reflect upon and learn from as they reexamine the struggles, the controversies, and the conflicts of the Civil Rights Movement. Students of history need guidance in analyzing and reflecting upon racism and other forms of inequality that continue to exist. This unit of study presents the Civil Rights Era as a time of change, a time of leadership from everyday citizens as well as charismatic leaders, and a time of violence and nonviolence, both of which became tools for change. The uncomfortable realities of the Civil Rights Movement are presented in the words of those who experienced it, in the dramatic pictures that capture unforgettable scenes of strength and violence, and in the collective actions of the people, many of them children and youth. An understanding of the Civil Rights Movement must go beyond the classic few heroes who are celebrated during Black History month. The Civil Rights Movement, still etched in the memory of many older citizens who lived during that time, is a legacy that our young children deserve to experience through the eyes of those who came before them. They need to connect what happened then to contemporary issues.

This unit considers the rights and responsibilities of democratic citizens more clearly defined and honored as a result of the Civil Rights Movement. This unit of study has been developed to support students' thinking through what happened, why it happened, and the forces (political, social, and economic) that made it happen. In every lesson, students are asked to step into the world of the time period, to hear about and to see what was happening, to read the words of real people and to imagine their hopes, dreams, and feelings. Students also learn to question the accounts left behind and to recognize different perspectives on a singular event (historiography). Working like historians, students uncover information as they sort through evidence from the past and then connect it to what they already know. As they experience each lesson's activities, they are asked to take a careful look at the participants in the movement and align them with the expectations for democratic citizenship (forms of protest).

Engaging With History in the Classroom: The Civil Rights Movement contains 12 lessons, one of which encompasses 2 days of activity by design. Other lessons may be condensed or expanded to meet pacing and scheduling needs. The unit can be completed in approximately 3 weeks or about 20 hours of learning time.

In Lesson 1, What Do You Know About the Civil Rights Movement?, students view images of the Civil Rights Movement and then work in small groups to review what they know and develop questions they have about this period in history. Students also complete a preassessment to gauge their present knowledge about the Civil Rights Movement.

In Lesson 2, How Did Individuals and Groups Build Momentum for Change?, students analyze the role of the National Association for the Advancement of Colored People (NAACP) in challenging school segregation. Working in groups, students examine the *Brown v. Board of Education* (1954) decision and the court cases under *Brown v. Board of Education*. They also examine political cartoons as historical evidence.

In Lesson 3, What Was the Impact of *Brown v. Board of Education* on Individuals and Communities?, students read and listen to interviews of people who experienced the desegregation of public schools. They learn the process of preparing for an oral history, interviewing selected people, and recording the oral history for an audience (video, audio tape, written notes).

In Lesson 4, Was *Brown v. Board of Education* Successful?, students participate in a Structured Academic Controversy focused on the key question, "Was *Brown v. Board of Education* Successful?" Students consider both sides of the controversy, analyzing both the short-term and long-term effects of the court decision.

In Lesson 5, What Is Leadership in a Democratic Society?, students analyze historical records of the Montgomery Bus Boycott and use a concept development strategy to examine the concepts of democratic citizenship and boycott.

In Lesson 6, How Can Conflict Be Resolved Without Violence? students analyze Dr. Martin Luther King Jr.'s "Letter From Birmingham Jail." On day 1, students read and analyze Dr. Martin Luther King Jr.'s letter. On day 2, students engage in a Socratic Seminar, considering Dr. King's words and actions in relation to the expectations for democratic citizens and his impact on the quest for equal rights.

In Lesson 7, Can Children Be Change Agents for Equal Rights?, students view the video *Mighty Times: The Children's March* and record personal reflections on what happened. They analyze their feelings about the events and share their impressions in a class discussion.

In Lesson 8, How Did Social and Legal Interventions Intersect in the Fight for Civil Rights?, students analyze artwork depicting civil rights issues. Next students examine three important interventions that were used to ensure the civil rights of all citizens:

➤ federal action to enforce voting rights,
➤ legislation including the Civil Rights Act of 1964 and the Voting Rights Act of 1965, and
➤ nonviolent protests and their impact.

In Lesson 9, Moderation or Militancy: Is a Choice Necessary?, students compare and contrast the messages and methods of Dr. Martin Luther King Jr. and Malcolm X. They explore the actions of both men in relation to an Escalation Model for examining political actions in protest.

In Lesson 10, What Is a Movement?, students analyze descriptions of historic events to determine the essential elements of a movement. In a jigsaw format, students explore specific examples of movements including the Women's Movement and the American Indian Movement.

In Lesson 11, Who Works for Social Justice?, students work in small groups to select a contemporary social justice issue, complete research on their selected social justice issue, and identify key points. Next students develop a format for presenting their cause to the class audience.

In Lesson 12, What Have We Learned About the Civil Rights Movement?, students share stories, poems, and personal ideas about social, economic, or political social justice issues worthy of attention. Finally, students reflect on what they have learned and demonstrate their progress through a postassessment.

CIVIL RIGHTS UNIT PROJECTS

We suggest incorporating a project that encompasses the entire unit as a way for students to learn how to explore a topic in depth and to communicate their findings to an audience. Several options for unit projects are discussed below.

Reading discussion groups. Reading discussion groups may be introduced as an optional, parallel activity for the duration of this unit. Adding the dimension of reading and talking about historical narratives has multiple benefits. Students can envision more of the story of the Civil Rights Movement as they think about the human side of the critical events, the lifestyles, and the struggles of people. Just as historians are evidence gatherers and interpreters, students are asked to find examples of historical facts in the readings and then to check these facts for accuracy both singularly and in the context of the actual events. Students find role models within the historical novels and are better able to envision people of their age enduring circumstances unlike theirs yet representative of the human struggle.

The historical reading discussion groups teach skills of reading fluency and comprehension, thus supporting essential language arts expectations. For struggling readers, the story aspect of the narrative provides more context for the understanding of historical passages required as unit readings. For students learning the English language, the variety of novels enables the teacher to assign books with appropriate readability levels and interests. The analysis of vocabulary built into the reading discussion assignment structure also supports language learning. For students ready for advanced assignments, the options for reading material and the complexity of some of the choices and topics enables them to go beyond their current knowledge with the added benefit of personal choice.

Guidelines for managing and conducting the reading discussion groups are included in Handout 0.2. The reading groups may be part of the language arts block of the school day and/ or may be directed by the teacher of language arts as a parallel, interdisciplinary assignment.

Oral histories. Lesson 3 introduces students to oral histories and asks small groups to develop and share an oral history of someone who has memories of the Civil Rights Movement. You may choose to guide your students in conducing one or more oral histories, in small groups, as a class, or as individuals. Guidelines for Oral Histories are included in Handout 0.3.

Biographies. The study of the Civil Rights Movement can be enriched by a deeper analysis of some people whose names are little mentioned but whose contributions to the movement were critical in ensuring effective changes. Students may write brief biographies of selected individuals, adding photos, documents, and timelines. Another option is to have students create biographical trading cards. Each student is assigned an individual for whom they will create a trading card (two-sided) that contains graphics on one side and bulleted information about the person on the other. The card deck project may be added to at the end of each lesson or may be built at some point as a homework project. These cards can be duplicated on cardstock and then used for review or playing games, which students will enjoy creating.

Class online sharing about civil rights. A number of software options are available online for developing class sites for sharing learning activities, research, reports, and topics of interest. You may already have or may choose to develop a class webpage, blog, or wiki. One very flexible program for sharing can be found at padlet.com. Padlet allows the user to create a blank "wall" and then drag and drop links, videos, comments, files, or projects related to the topic so they can be organized and easily accessed and shared with others securely. Student groups or individuals can create a wall on a specific topic or event for sharing with small groups or the class. Student's oral histories would be well suited to a presence on a Padlet site and can be set for secure access.

Arts museum of the Civil Rights Movement. Invite students to locate works of art and music to contribute to a class museum. Plan for an event and invite adults and other classes to come to the museum at a certain time. Ask students to serve as docents, preparing ahead of time to explain the significance of their selected work of art or music. This museum could also be "translated" into an online museum placed on a class or school web page. Great sources for ideas can be found at:

> Oh Freedom: Teaching African American Civil Rights Through American Art at the Smithsonian: http://africanamericanart.si.edu/art

> The Power of Imagery in Advancing Civil Rights: http://www.smithsonianmag.com/arts-culture/the-power-of-imagery-in-advancing-civil-rights-72983041/#3cwfglMSt3z VYAdX.99

HANDOUT 0.1
SUGGESTED BOOKS FOR READING AND DISCUSSION OF THE CIVIL RIGHTS MOVEMENT

The $66 Summer: A Novel of the Segregated South by John Armistead
It is the summer of 1955 in Obadiah, AL, and George, a 13-year-old White boy, is working in his grandmother's store to save money to buy a motorcycle. He becomes friends with Esther and her brother Bennett, two "colored" children who live nearby. These three adventure-seeking friends sneak onto the property of Mr. Vorhise, a bigoted man who raises fighting dogs. George begins to think about the mysterious departure of Staple, Esther and Bennett's father, in light of the stories he hears from friends and relatives. He must confront the realities of racism as he and his friends uncover some chilling evidence of tragic events.

Brown Girl Dreaming by Jacqueline Woodson
What was it really like to be a Black child growing up during the time of the Civil Rights Movement? In this beautiful memoir written in verse, Jacqueline Woodson tells her story, contrasting her experiences living in South Carolina and then in Brooklyn, NY. Lovers of poetry and stories of real family life will treasure this book.

Claudette Colvin: Twice Toward Justice by Phillip Hoose (Biography)
On March 2, 1955, 15-year-old Claudette Colvin refused to give up her seat to a White woman on a segregated bus in Montgomery, AL, and was arrested. Unlike Rosa Parks's celebrated bus ride, Claudette's action was met with harsh responses from her classmates as well as from leaders in the community. This book is based on interviews with Claudette Colvin as well as others who were part of the Montgomery Bus Boycott and the court case that challenged segregation in Montgomery and led to the elimination of Jim Crow laws.

Devil on My Heels by Joyce McDonald
Dove Alderman, 15, is the White daughter of an orange grower in Florida who makes some upsetting discoveries about her community and her family as she views the mistreatment of the orange pickers who are African American and Mexican immigrants. This story of suspense graphically shows the confrontations and violence that occurred in the 1950s in one small town as old ideas and young people's unwillingness to accept them clash amid ongoing mistreatment and prejudice.

Fire From the Rock by Sharon Draper
In 1957, Sylvia is asked to join a small group of Black students in integrating Central High School in Little Rock, AR. Recognizing the need for change and the challenge to young people to get involved, Sylvia decides to leave her familiar school and community surroundings. At first, she views the move as an exciting honor but quickly discovers the danger and hostility for herself and the other Black students as the town's hostility grows and violence escalates. Sylvia must choose between a nonviolent approach or aggression.

The Girl From the Tar Paper School: Barbara Rose Johns and the Advent of the Civil Rights Movement by Teri Kanefield (Biography)
This biographical view of one teenager who became a leader in the Civil Rights Movement highlights the way in which nonviolence was ultimately effective. Barbara led the first public protest of unfair conditions in segregated schools. She and other students conducted a walkout to protest the unfair conditions in their school. In spite of

Handout 0.1: Suggested Books for Reading and Discussion of the Civil Rights Movement, continued

the ridicule from the school officials, local news, and White citizens, Barbara and her fellow classmates remained true to their cause. Eventually the students' efforts became one of the court cases that were part of *Brown v. Board of Education*. The book includes many photos, news clips, and other documents.

Just Like Martin by Ossie Davis
Isaac Stone ("Stone"), 14, wants to join a church group for the Freedom March on Washington, DC, but his father, a war veteran, does not agree with his son's belief in the nonviolent approach to the resolution of racial inequities. Stone's eagerness to follow the lead of Dr. Martin Luther King Jr. is tested when two classmates die in a bomb explosion of his Alabama church. Responding to the senseless violence he and his friends witness, Stone organizes a peaceful children's march. His father, still struggling with his own feelings contrasted with the efforts of his son, must confront their differences.

Mr. Touchdown by Lyda Phillips
Unexpectedly, Eddie Russell, a high school football star, and his younger sister Lakeesha become part of the Civil Rights Movement in Memphis, TN, when they discover that their father, Reverend Henry Russell, has agreed to enroll them in the all-White high school, joining two other Black students in the integration effort. At first, they encounter only passive racism but the taunting and tormenting behaviors of White students and faculty escalate and ultimately result in an assault on Lakeesha and Eddie's struggle with his commitment to nonviolence. The story is based upon the author's real-life experiences as a teenager.

One Crazy Summer by Rita Williams-Garcia
It is 1968 and Delphine, 11, is sent with her two younger sisters to spend the summer with their birth mother, Cecile, who long ago abandoned them. Traveling from Brooklyn, NY, to Oakland, CA, the girls anticipate a time of fun in the sun with trips to Disneyland and Hollywood. Imagine their surprise when their mother appears less than happy to have them and sends them to the community day camp run by the Black Panthers. Delphine tells the story of how the sisters observe the need for social change and learn about the efforts of the Panthers to protect the rights of Black citizens during a time of tumult.

The Return of Gabriel by John Armistead
Enjoying a summer vacation together is the most important goal for two young teens, Cooper and Jubal, living in segregated Mississippi. In spite of their racial differences, the boys have much in common as neighbors and friends. It is 1964, Freedom Summer, and college students from California come to town to bring change to the town by supporting Black citizens and encourage them to vote. Suddenly Cooper is caught in the middle between his father's support of the KKK and his loyalties to his African American friends and neighbors. Cooper puts himself in danger as he and Jubal struggle with the racial tensions around them and their determination to remain friends.

Revolution by Deborah Wiles
Two young residents of a town in Mississippi experience the changes coming to their everyday life during Freedom Summer, 1964. Sunny, a 12-year-old White girl, is adjusting to family changes, including a new stepmother and her two children, and also begins to become aware of the bigger issues facing her community as Northern civil rights supporters come to register Black voters. Raymond is impatient to see changes happen in Jim Crow laws that bar him from many public places because of his color. The worlds of Sunny and Raymond intersect as they experience the horrible dangers present in the quest for equal rights.

Handout 0.1: Suggested Books for Reading and Discussion of the Civil Rights Movement, continued

The Rock and the River by Kekla Magoon

Sam is 14 and the son of a civil rights activist who is deeply involved in Martin Luther King Jr.'s call for nonviolent protest. Sam joins his family in peaceful demonstrations in 1968. When Sam discovers that his brother has joined the Black Panthers, Sam's thoughts are conflicted. When he witnesses the police brutally beating a friend, he questions both his father's approach to equal rights as well as the approach of the Black Panther party.

A Tugging String: A Novel About Growing Up During the Civil Rights Era by David Greenberg

The son of a civil rights lawyer working with Dr. Martin Luther King Jr., Duvy Greenberg, 12, is living in Great Neck, NY, far removed from the conflicts in the South. That is, until he comes to understand the dangers of his father's work and the courageous acts of the people his father seeks to help. With a focus on the Selma-Montgomery Voting Rights March, this book blends real events of the 1960s with the imagined world of one family. The author's father was a civil rights lawyer and director of the NAACP Legal Defense Fund in the 1960s.

Warriors Don't Cry: The Searing Memoir of the Battle to Integrate Little Rock's Central High by Melba Pattillo Beals (Biography)

The integration of Little Rock's Central High School in 1957 followed the 1954 Supreme Court *Brown v. Board of Education* decision. The author, Melba Pattillo Beals, tells her story as one of the "Little Rock Nine." These brave teenagers faced the climactic battle for school desegregation, experiencing taunts, threats from lynch mobs, and actual attacks. Melba shares her thoughts and feelings, describing in detail attacks on her and her fellow African American schoolmates. Her memoir is an inspiring story of courage and determination.

The Watsons Go to Birmingham–1963 by Christopher Curtis

Traveling from their happy home in Flint, MI, to Birminghan, AL to visit Grandma, the Watsons quickly become part of a different world as they encounter segregated restaurants and restrooms as well as different "requirements" for African American families like theirs. Kenny, the happy-go-lucky 10-year-old in the family of five, narrates the story, guiding us through the positive and negative aspects of being in the South in 1963. Experiencing the bombing of a local Baptist church, Kenny and his family recognize that their lives are forever changed.

HANDOUT 0.2
GUIDELINES FOR BOOK DISCUSSIONS

Historical fiction or historical biographies provide students a window into history. Effective historical fiction or biography is well-researched and based on historical evidence. To begin discussion groups in your classroom, offer students choices, asking them to select from several book options, either as individuals or in small groups. Provide students with brief book summaries prior to selections. Prepare a schedule for book discussion group meetings. A weekly meeting is productive, allowing students time for reading and research prior to the meeting.

In preparation for each discussion, provide 1–3 guiding questions for students. Be sure the questions require students to think as opposed to finding a simple fact. Keep in mind that the basic purpose of the questions is to stimulate discussion based on a critical analysis of the reading. Good questions should demand responses that encompass a problem, an issue, or a comparison; trace a feeling or pattern of action; or show a trend over an entire section of the book. Questions should be at the analysis level in which the learner is asked to identify several passages from the reading that offer evidence to support the learner's response. Students should be required to compare, contrast, categorize, take apart, or in some way show a deep understanding, well beyond finding the "correct" answer. Some examples of good guiding questions include:

> Cite several passages to show Jim's feelings about his involvement in the protest.
> Which character showed the most aggression in this section? What do you feel caused this behavior?
> What were people's attitudes toward _____? How did they justify their actions and feelings?
> They say "Beauty is in the eye of the beholder." How does this apply to the section you have just read?
> In what way do you see Rosa's actions as being "out of character" for her?
> Can you find an example of democratic citizenship in this chapter?

Students are capable of developing their own questions within each discussion group. You, as the teacher, can review their proposed questions for the next reading and approve or suggest modifications. Questions requiring reasoning and evidence are the key to deep thought.

Students should maintain a novel notebook in which they record each question and the page, paragraph, and comments for the discussion on one page and the page, paragraph, word, and definition for new words met in the reading on another page. This is the key preparation for each meeting.

For each discussion session, students should also locate and record incidences of historical facts contained in the reading, citing the page and paragraph to share with the group. Students should also verify these historical facts prior to the discussion, enabling the group to learn how closely the author remained true to recorded history about the events, setting, and characters.

The discussion circle is student directed and evaluated. The teacher observes the interaction and serves as a guide as needed. Students take turns being the discussion leader, starting off the discussion with a question, a search for historical facts, or clarifications of words used in the text.

A book discussion should always end with an individual reflection on the success of the discussion and the contributions made to the group. Areas of consideration should include preparation of responses to discussion questions and vocabulary entries, participation in the discussion, listening and connecting to others, and research on the match of historical comments in the book to actual history. A more direct assessment may be used, asking students to rate themselves and their discussion group, using a scale of 1 (low) to 5 (high) for each element considered including preparation, participation, connections, and historical research. After the numerical ratings, both individual and groups should decide what could be done to improve their next book discussion.

HANDOUT 0.3
GUIDELINES FOR ORAL HISTORIES

KEY STEPS IN THE ORAL HISTORY PROCESS

1. Establish the purpose for and scope of the oral history project.
2. Complete preliminary research about the topic.
3. Identify potential list of persons to interview.
4. Develop key interview questions.
5. Determine methods to be used.
6. Train interviewers in effective practices.
7. Schedule interviews and attain permission for use.
8. Complete transcript of interviews.
9. Publish interviews.

TIPS FOR TEACHERS

1. Decide on the number of interviews you want to guide and supervise:
   a. **Whole-class interview project.** You may decide to make the project a whole-class activity. In this case, you would help students to identify and select two to three people to interview who will illuminate the area of interest. Groups of students take charge of various tasks in preparation for the interviews, in planning, scheduling, and conducting the interviews, and in managing the recording and publication of the interviews.
   b. **Small-group interview project.** Another option would be for each small group of students to assume responsibility for one interview, completing all of the required activities within their group. This option may be limited by the amount of time available and the number of persons available to be interviewed.
   c. **Individual student interview project.** You may choose to allow selected students who volunteer or are assigned as an extension project the responsibility for an individual interview.

2. Ensure that your students acquire sufficient background information about the topic to enable them to develop effective questions and to be able to interpret the thoughts and feelings of those interviewed in the context of the overall topic.
3. Guide students in identifying people who may have personal experiences related to the topic. Ask students in what ways these potential interviewees might be motivated to take part in the project. What community groups or contacts might assist in identifying key people?
4. Ask students to suggest many potential interview questions. Then ask them to check each question against the purpose and goals of the project. Will the question lead to many possible responses? Is the question too narrow? Remind students that they will need background data on the persons interviewed as well as their stories and feelings regarding their experiences. From many questions, help students to narrow the possibilities and develop a final set of questions.
5. Help students to determine how information will be captured. Will notes be taken? Audio recordings? Video recordings?

Handout 0.3: Guidelines for Oral Histories, continued

6. Guide students in practice sessions that are simulations of actual interviews, using the selected questions and recording methods. Check results and make adjustments as needed. Ask students to make a list of helpful hints for interviewers.

7. Make plans for the persons to be interviewed. Who? When? Where? How will they be invited? What permissions are needed? How will they be welcomed and made comfortable? Who will share the goals of the project? How will they be thanked for participation?

8. Conduct the interviews and arrange for transcripts to be maintained, analyzed, and shared. Decide on a storage and retrieval process.

9. Publish interviews in an appropriate way, recognizing the value of the results. Should they be accessible to the persons interviewed? To others in the school community? Available in the library? Other community groups?

SUGGESTED RESOURCES

➤ Wood, L. (2001). *Oral history projects in your classroom.* Atlanta, GA: Oral History Association.

➤ http://www.oralhistory.org/web-guides-to-doing-oral-history/

➤ http://dohistory.org/on_your_own/toolkit/oralHistory.html

LESSON 1
WHAT DO YOU KNOW ABOUT THE CIVIL RIGHTS MOVEMENT?

OVERVIEW

LESSON AT A GLANCE

➤ Students view images of the Civil Rights Movement and then work in small groups to review what they know and develop questions they have about this period in history.

➤ Students complete a preassessment to gauge their present knowledge about the Civil Rights Movement.

TIMELINE EVENTS

➤ 1857: Dred Scott sued for his freedom
➤ 1861: Civil War began
➤ 1863: Lincoln signed the Emancipation Proclamation
➤ 1865: Civil War ended
➤ 1865: Freedman's Bureau established
➤ 1865: Ku Klux Klan organized
➤ 1865: Thirteenth Amendment ratified
➤ 1868: Fourteenth Amendment ratified
➤ 1870: Fifteenth Amendment ratified
➤ 1870: First Jim Crow law passed in Tennessee
➤ 1875: First Civil Rights Act passed
➤ 1883: Civil Rights Act of 1875 struck down
➤ 1896: *Plessy v. Ferguson* established separate but equal doctrine
➤ 1910: National Association for the Advancement of Colored People (NAACP) founded
➤ 1948: President Truman signed an executive order declaring a policy of equal treatment and opportunity for all persons in the armed services

ESSENTIAL QUESTIONS

➤ How did Jim Crow laws influence racial segregation in the South?
➤ Does racial equality depend upon government action?
➤ Did African Americans attain the American Dream by the early 20th century?

CONCEPTUAL UNDERSTANDINGS

➤ The United States Constitution and the Declaration of Independence are grounded in the idea of liberty and justice for all people.

➤ In spite of the Emancipation Proclamation and the 13th, 14th, and 15th Amendments, thousands of African Americans remained in positions of forced labor for decades.

➤ The South remained the main, but not the only, area of victimization for African Americans and other groups.

➤ Oppression of African Americans was political, social, and cultural in nature.

IMPORTANT TERMS AND IDEAS

➤ *movement:* a group of people working together toward a common goal

➤ *segregation:* the separation of people based on race

➤ *prejudice:* a bias that keeps someone from being fair

➤ *discrimination:* unfair treatment based on a certain characteristic such as race

➤ *intimidation:* purposely inciting fear in someone

MATERIALS

➤ Collection of historical documents (photos, news clippings, narratives, videos) related to the Civil Rights Movement. Sources:
  • http://life.time.com/civil-rights-movement/
  • http://www.pbs.org/wgbh/amex/eyesontheprize/resources/res_img.html
  • http://www.cnn.com/2014/04/07/us/gallery/iconic-civil-rights/

➤ Civil Rights Era music: http://www.folkways.si.edu/voices-of-the-civil-rights-movement-black-american-freedom-songs-1960-1966/african-american-music-documentary-struggle-protest/album/smithsonian

➤ Audio of Civil Rights songs, testimonials, and speeches from *Sing for Freedom: The Story of the Civil Rights Movement Through Its Songs.* Washington, DC: Smithsonian Folkways Records (includes extensive notes; available for purchase from http://www.folkways.si.edu/sing-for-freedom-the-story-of-the-civil-rights-movement/african-american-music-american-history-historical-song-struggle-protest/album/smithsonian)

➤ Mural paper and markers for a graffiti wall

➤ Markers

➤ Chart paper labeled Who, What, When, Where, Why for each small group

➤ Handout 1.1: Civil Rights Movement Preassessment

➤ Handout 1.2: Key Questions for Civil Rights Movement Unit (prepared as a display chart)

SUGGESTED RESOURCES

➤ Adelman, B., & Johnson, C. (2007). *Mine eyes have seen: Bearing witness to the Civil Rights struggle.* New York, NY: Time.

➤ McWhorter, D. (2004). *A dream of freedom*. New York, NY: Scholastic.

➤ Morris, A. D. (1998). *The origins of the Civil Rights Movement*. New York, NY: Free Press.

➤ http://www.civilrightsteaching.org

➤ http://www.pbs.org/wgbh/amex/eyesontheprize/resources/res_img.html

➤ http://www.gilderlehrman.org/history-by-era/1945-present/civil-rights-movement

➤ http://www.pbs.org/tpt/slavery-by-another-name/watch/

➤ https://www.facinghistory.org/for-educators/educator-resources/resource-collections/civil-rights-resource-collection

➤ http://www.loc.gov/teachers/classroommaterials/presentationsandactivities/presentations/civil-rights/

INSTRUCTIONS

THE HOOK

1. Prepare a display of historical documents and photos about the Civil Rights Movement. Show documents a few days prior to the beginning of the unit in a way suitable for your classroom. You may want to present these as a bulletin board, a center, or simply a collection in a box. Alternatively, you may prepare a timeline with key events and related photos or news clippings.

2. If time permits, show some of the PBS documentary, *Slavery by Another Name* (http://www.pbs.org/tpt/slavery-by-another-name/watch), as an introduction to the unit. Preview this powerful documentary prior to showing and select a clip that will enable you to begin the discussion of the time period between the Emancipation Proclamation and the beginning of the Civil Rights Movement of the 1950s and 1960s. If you do not have sufficient class time, be sure to watch the documentary for your own background knowledge. The PBS site also includes tips for facilitating classroom discussion of this sensitive topic (http://pbs.bento.storage.s3.amazonaws.com/hostedbento-prod/filer_public/SBAN/Images/Classrooms/Ten%20Tips%20for%20Facilitating%20Classroom%20Discussions%20on%20Sensitive%20Topics_Final.pdf).

3. Play a Civil Rights Era song as students enter the room. Display a large piece of mural paper (to be kept for redisplay in the last lesson) for a graffiti wall. Provide students with markers and ask them to write words and phrases that come to mind when they hear the term "Civil Rights Movement." Allow a few minutes for everyone to have an opportunity to add something to the "Wall of Civil Rights." Tell students that this wall will be something you will keep as a record of the beginning of their study and that you will post it again on the last day of the unit to see what they then think of their words.

4. Next tell students that you would like them to complete a preassessment. Assure students that a preassessment is simply a way for you and them to know what they have already learned and what they still need to learn. Let them know that the preassessment is not graded. You may use the following script or discuss preassessments in your own way: *Today we will begin our study of the Civil Rights Movement. First you will complete a preassessment, sometimes called a pretest. Do you recall a time when you took a pretest for a class? What is the purpose of a pretest? Your responses to the preassessment will help me to*

plan better learning activities for you. It will show what you already know and what you will need to learn. You may find some questions on the preassessment that you just don't know how to answer. Some questions are asking you to think deeply and not just give a "correct" answer like a name, date, or yes/no. If you are stumped, you should make an attempt, recording any ideas you think are related, even if it is a guess.

5. Distribute copies of the Civil Rights Movement Preassessment (Handout 1.1) and allow students time to complete it. Let students know that you will give them feedback on the preassessments and that at the end of the unit they will have an opportunity to show you and themselves how much they have learned.

DEVELOPING CONCEPTUAL UNDERSTANDING

6. Tell students that they will work in small groups to record their knowledge about the struggle for civil rights in America. Encourage them to think about people and events they have already studied during their earlier lessons in American history, especially those that focused on the rights of African Americans. Ask them also to consider the Civil Rights Movement that occurred in the 1950s and 1960s.

7. Provide each group with chart paper labeled Who, What, When, Where, Why and ask them to record what the group thinks they know about the struggle for civil rights for all United States citizens. Let them know that they may list any ideas, names, dates, and details they can think of. Tell students they will have about 10 minutes to record some of their ideas.

8. Circulate as groups discuss and record what they know. If students aren't readily remembering connections from their past studies, remind them of a few key people and events such as *Plessy v. Ferguson* with its establishment of de jure segregation; the 13th, 14th, and 15th Amendment rights; and the creation of Jim Crow laws and the ways in which these laws caused the steady erosion of African Americans' rights. The Civil Rights Movement is, in this way, closely related to students' prior learning.

9. After the work period, ask groups to display their charts and guide a discussion of student responses. Encourage students to add items as they come to mind over the next few days. Be sure to consider student responses that might require clarification, correction, further discussion, or research to avoid inaccuracies. Ask students to help you develop a simple timeline of the most significant events they have recorded such as the Dred Scott Decision; Civil War; Emancipation Proclamation; 13th, 14th, and 15th amendments; Jim Crow laws; Civil Rights Act of 1875; *Plessy v. Ferguson*; and the founding of NAACP.

SOAR: SUMMARIZE, OBSERVE, ASSESS, REFLECT

10. Following the discussion, ask students to think about the issues of civil rights. Ask them what they wonder about and what they are interested in learning more about regarding the Civil Rights Movement. Record their questions and let them know that these and other questions you have prepared will be the focus of their study. Let them know that they will be learning some very important things about this period of change for all Americans.

11. Display the students' questions as well as the chart you have prepared with the unit questions (Handout 1.2). You may wish to distribute copies of the unit questions, asking students to add their own to the list. Refer to these charts throughout the unit to keep a focus on important ideas. Remind students to add items to their group charts as they get new ideas.

THINK AGAIN: HOMEWORK

12. Ask students to record an example of one right they have as citizens of the United States and one right that they know some people did not have in the past.

KEEP ON GOING: LESSON EXTENSIONS

13. Encourage students to locate additional images and art representative of the Civil Rights Movement to contribute to the class display.
14. Assign students who may need additional challenges the task of developing a timeline with key events of the Civil Rights Movement to display, adding key items throughout the unit including photos, quotes, and summaries.

HANDOUT 1.1
CIVIL RIGHTS MOVEMENT PREASSESSMENT

1. Think of individuals, groups, or events that made significant contributions to the Civil Rights Movement. Record what you know for each one you choose.

Person, Group, or Event	Contributions/Results

2. The Civil Rights Movement includes many examples of conflict. For each generalization about conflict listed below, describe a situation that occurred during the Civil Rights Movement.

Conflict arises from differences in people's beliefs, needs, values, or practices.	
Conflict resolution may be violent or nonviolent.	
Conflict may support political, social, or economic change.	

Handout 1.1: Civil Rights Movement Preassessment, continued

3. Congratulations! You have been hired as a historian to write a new book about the Civil Rights Movement. You want to be sure to focus on democratic citizenship. Tell about two examples of democratic citizenship you will select to include in your book.

HANDOUT 1.2
KEY QUESTIONS FOR CIVIL RIGHTS MOVEMENT UNIT

➤ What actions had an impact on the initial steps toward the Civil Rights Movement?

➤ What were the goals of the Civil Rights Movement?

➤ In what ways did schools and other public places move from segregation to integration?

➤ Which groups and individuals led the way for civil rights?

➤ What were the major strategies used during the Civil Rights Movement by different groups?

➤ What were the roles of different groups and institutions?

➤ What were some key events in the Civil Rights Movement?

➤ Why was there so much resistance to civil rights in many parts of the country?

➤ What led to the Civil Rights Movement's successes in the 1950s and 1960s?

➤ What has been the overall impact of the Civil Rights Movement?

LESSON 2
HOW DID INDIVIDUALS AND GROUPS BUILD MOMENTUM FOR CHANGE?

OVERVIEW

LESSON AT A GLANCE

➤ Students analyze the role of the National Association for the Advancement of Colored People (NAACP) in challenging school segregation.

➤ Working in groups, students examine the *Brown v. Board of Education* decision and the court cases under *Brown v. Board of Education*.

➤ Students discuss political cartoons as historical evidence.

TIMELINE EVENTS

➤ 1909: National Association for the Advancement of Colored People (NAACP) founded

➤ 1935: NAACP begins challenging inequality of segregated schools

➤ 1938: NAACP begins winning cases for equal access to graduate schools

➤ 1939: Thurgood Marshall named special counsel for NAACP

➤ 1949: *Briggs et al. v. Elliot* in South Carolina

➤ 1950: *Bolling v. Sharpe* in Washington, D.C.

➤ 1951: *Benton v. Gebhart* and *Bulah v. Gebhart* in Delaware

➤ 1951: *Davis et al. v. School Board of Prince Edward County, VA*

➤ 1951: *Brown v. Board of Education* in Topeka, KS

➤ 1952: *Brown v. Board of Education* cases become collective (five cases)

➤ 1954: *Brown v. Board of Education* decision

➤ 1955: Supreme Court remedies in *Brown II*

ESSENTIAL QUESTIONS

➤ How did schooling differ for African American and White children in the 1950s?

➤ How could an organization like the NAACP influence the political and social patterns that sought to maintain segregation?

➤ In what ways can the legal process change the political and social patterns that resulted in segregation?

CONCEPTUAL UNDERSTANDINGS

➤ In spite of the Emancipation Proclamation and the passing of the 13th, 14th, and 15th Amendments, segregation was deeply rooted in American society until the 1950s.

➤ Change occurs through varied forces including individual and group actions as well as government interventions.

➤ Individual and group protests became expressions of a division among people regarding segregation. Such protests were the beginning of a movement.

➤ The impact of inequality in education became a cause requiring more direct measures in Southern states. Supported by the NAACP, several cases seeking an end to segregation and equal education were brought before the courts.

IMPORTANT TERMS AND IDEAS

➤ *separate but equal:* policy allowing segregation of Blacks but supposedly ensuring equal opportunities or equal quality

➤ *grass roots:* arising from the common people

➤ *precedent:* an example cited in later similar instances, generally prior court decisions

➤ *et al.:* and others

➤ *testimony:* a witness statement in court

➤ *psychological damage:* trauma to the mind, often because of troubling experiences

➤ *tangible:* real, concrete

➤ *intangible:* unable to be seen or sensed

➤ *suit:* formal complaint brought to a court of law

➤ *depose:* to testify, usually in a written statement

➤ *landmark case:* a legal decision of great historic significance

➤ *plaintiff:* someone who brings a lawsuit in a court case

➤ *defendant:* person being sued in court

➤ *appeal:* to seek a different outcome, especially in a court case

➤ *equalization:* the act of making treatment equal

MATERIALS

➤ Political cartoons to project: http://www.streetlaw.org/en/Page.Landmark.Brown.act.cartoon.aspx

➤ Handout 2.1: Photographs of Two Schools in South Carolina, 1950

➤ Handout 2.2: Reenactment Script: *Brown v. Board of Education* Decision

➤ Handout 2.3: The Road to *Brown v. Board of Education*

➤ Handout 2.4: 1951: *Davis et al. v. County School Board of Prince Edward County, VA*

➤ Handout 2.5: 1952: *Belton v. Gebhart* and *Bulah v. Gebhart*, Claymont and Hockessin, DE

➤ Handout 2.6: 1951: *Briggs et al. v. Elliott et al.*, Clarendon County, SC

➤ Handout 2.7: 1950: *Bolling v. Sharpe*, Washington, DC

➤ Handout 2.8: 1951: *Brown v. Board of Education*, Topeka, KS

➤ Handout 2.9: Notes on *Brown v. Board of Education* Court Cases

➤ Handout 2.10: *Brown v. Board of Education* Majority Opinion Excerpts

➤ Handout 2.11: *Brown II* Majority Opinion Excerpts

SUGGESTED RESOURCES

➤ McKissack, P. (2007). *A friendship for today.* New York, NY: Scholastic.

➤ Perez, L. K. (2007). *Remember as you pass me by.* Minneapolis, MN: Milkweed Editions.

➤ Dudley, M. (1994). *Brown v. Board of Education: School desegregation.* Minneapolis, MN: Twenty-First Century Books.

➤ Good, D. (2007). *Brown v. Board of Education: (Cornerstones of freedom).* New York, NY: Children's Press.

➤ McNeese, T. (2006). *Brown v. Board of Education: Integrating America's schools.* New York, NY: Chelsea House.

➤ Pierce, A. (2004). *Brown v. Board of Education.* Edina, MN: ABDO Publishing.

➤ Stokes, J. A. (2008). *Students on strike: Jim Crow, civil rights, Brown, and me.* Washington, DC: National Geographic.

➤ Tackach, J. (1998). *Brown v. Board of Education.* San Diego, CA: Lucent.

➤ http://www.pbslearningmedia.org/resource/osi04.soc.ush.civil.marshallsj/simple-justice-5-marshalls-closing-statement/

➤ http://sites.bergen.org/ourstory/projects/separate_BOE/index.htm

➤ http://www.nps.gov/NR/twhp/wwwlps/lessons/121brown/index.htm

➤ http://www.loc.gov/exhibits/brown/

➤ http://www.naacp.org/

➤ http://americanhistory.si.edu/brown/index.html

INSTRUCTIONS

Prior to beginning this lesson, make summary comments about the class's performance on the preassessment from Lesson 1, noting areas where many students shared knowledge of past events related to the Civil Rights Movement and general areas of study that they will begin to investigate during the unit.

> *Teacher's Note.* This lesson includes a reenactment of *Brown v. Board of Education* (Handout 2.2). Assign students to parts in the reenactment ahead of time and provide some practice time for this oral reading.

THE HOOK

1. Project pictures of segregated schools (Handout 2.1) and tell students that these two schools were in the same town in 1950. Ask, "Which school would you rather attend?" Ask students what they think people in the town would say about these two schools if they could speak to the school board. Would everyone have the same opinion? Continue the discussion, asking why the schools would be so different in the same town. Let students know these schools were in South Carolina in 1950. Tell students that today's lesson will involve more schools like this and more information about how people felt about them.

DEVELOPING CONCEPTUAL UNDERSTANDING

2. Write several sets of initials familiar to the students NFL, NBC, BSA/GSA. End your list with the initials of your school and ask students to tell you what each of these sets of initials stands for (National Football League, National Broadcasting Company, Boy Scouts of America/Girl Scouts of America). Then ask students if they belong to any groups or organizations that use initials as their identifier. Record a brief list of their contributions. Then write "NAACP" on the board and ask if anyone wants to guess the name of this organization, one that helped support desegregation in the United States. Students will likely guess "National" and "Association." Fill in the remainder of the words (National Association for the Advancement of Colored People) and ask what they think this organization might support. Ask if this name would be "politically correct" today. Ask, "Who Were the 'Colored' People?"

3. Tell students: *Could this name be considered offensive today? Well, someone asked the President of NAACP, Rev. William Barber, that very question in 2008 and how do you think he responded? This is what he said:*

> Great question. To be quite honest, there has been some internal wrestling with the name, but one reason it hasn't been changed is out of respect for history and the founders. In 1909, when the organization began, "colored" was one of the more respected identifications used by the larger society when compared with all the other grotesque names used to refer to African Americans. Another reason, however, is that the NAACP was founded as a multi-ethnic organization by whites, blacks, Jews, Christians, male, female, etc. In fact, the majority of the founders were white . . . So, in a sense, it was a "colored" organization dedicated to the eradication of racism and legalized racial discrimination and disparity. Even today, our mission is broad and covers all minorities.

4. Let students know that the NAACP is the primary organization that, over the past 100 years, has supported grassroots civil rights initiatives by focusing on legislative and judicial change. W.E.B. Du Bois was one of the founding members of the NAACP who, along with noted abolitionists, began this important organization that is still in existence today. Since its beginning, it has sought political, social, educational, and economic equality of minority group citizens of the United States and worked to eliminate racial prejudice. Tell students that one of the major accomplishments of the NAACP occurred in 1954 when the NAACP Legal Defense and Educational Fund provided legal counsel for the *Brown v. Board of Education* Supreme Court case that resulted in the outlawing of segregation in public schools.

5. Use Handout 2.2: Reenactment Script: *Brown v. Board of Education* Decision to introduce students to the Supreme Court decision in *Brown v. Board of Education*. Ask students to listen to the story of *Brown v. Board of Education* as the reenactment proceeds. Next provide students copies of Handout 2.3: The Road to *Brown v. Board of Education*. Ask students to read this background information about the NAACP's legal campaign and the legal battles preceding *Brown v. Board of Education*. You may choose to ask students to read and discuss the key events in small groups or read this information to the whole

class, pausing for discussion and questions. This background information will serve to help students situate the *Brown v. Board of Education* case in the context of the efforts of the NAACP to organize and fight for equality. You could also divide the separate bullets into sections/cards and provide small groups the set to place in the correct order and then discuss the events occurring over time, leading to the *Brown v. Board of Education* case. Additional information on the role of the NAACP can be found at the Smithsonian's Separate is Not Equal website: http://americanhistory.si.edu/brown/index.html. Some questions for discussion might include:

- What role did the NAACP play prior to *Brown v. Board of Education*?
- Why do you think the NAACP believed starting integration at the graduate school level was necessary?
- In what ways were the North and the South similar and different in terms of segregation?
- Why did the NAACP shift arguments from separate but equal does not exist to separate but equal is really unequal and denies citizen's rights?

6. Tell students that they will now examine each of the cases that came before the Supreme Court. Assign students to five small groups and provide a different case to each group (Handouts 2.4–2.8). Be sure students understand that these five cases collectively became the *Brown v. Board of Education* case. Consider the difficulty of the cases as you assign them to groups. From most difficult to easiest, the cases are: Virginia, Delaware, South Carolina, Washington, DC, and Kansas. Direct each group to read its case file sheet and prepare a summary of the information for sharing, using Handout 2.9: Notes on *Brown v. Board of Education* Court Cases as a guide for the information they prepare to share with the class. Internet links are provided for each case and, depending on the time allotted, can be used by the groups to extend their learning about the case assigned.

7. Circulate among the groups, checking for comprehension and asking key questions as needed to help students understand the facts of their case as they prepare their presentation. Be sure students emphasize the major facts of the case, the processes through the justice system, and the reasons they were included in the *Brown v. Board of Education* case. Once groups have had sufficient time to prepare, ask them to present their findings to the class. As each group presents, classmates should fill in their Notes on *Brown v. Board of Education* Court Cases handout (Handout 2.9). Ask students to discuss why these cases were considered together by the Supreme Court. Tell them that the Supreme Court made their decision based on evidence across all of the cases. Ask students to reflect on the impact of the Supreme Court decision that separate schools were not equal, and that schools must be integrated with all deliberate speed. Work with students to make a list of all of the possible problems that would now exist because of this court decision. Remind students that the impact was significant in the Southern states.

SOAR: SUMMARIZE, OBSERVE, ASSESS, REFLECT

8. Project one of the political cartoons from Street Law's Landmark Cases site for class viewing (see http://www.streetlaw.org/en/Page.Landmark.Brown.act.cartoon.aspx). You may need to review the idea of political cartoons as historical evidence to ensure that stu-

dents understand that the cartoons provide information and present a particular point of view. Ask:

- What do you see? What did you notice first?
- Can you find any symbols in the cartoon?
- Did the artist use any words to support the message?
- What is the big issue presented here?
- Did the artist make any comparisons in the piece?
- What is the artist's message?

9. Clarify the message of the cartoon for students as needed.

10. Encourage students to focus on the issues presented in the cartoon and the work of the NAACP as they participate in the day's activities. Use think-pair-share to have students respond to these questions:

- What is the role of the Supreme Court?
- What does it mean to appeal a court decision?
- Does the Supreme Court hear all appeals from lower courts?

11. Remind students of the 14th Amendment and *Plessy v. Ferguson*. Make sure they remember the "separate but equal" doctrine.

THINK AGAIN: HOMEWORK

12. Provide half of the students with Handout 2.10: *Brown v. Board of Education* Majority Opinion Excerpts and the other half with Handout 2.11: *Brown II* Majority Opinion Excerpts. Explain that, because the first decision did not provide information to the states on how to implement the Supreme Court decision or when it should happen, *Brown II* was a decision that addressed these issues. Tell students to read their assigned paper and prepare to explain to someone who read the other majority opinion (*Brown I* or *Brown II*) two key points provided by the courts. Begin the next lesson with a few minutes of peer sharing on these two majority opinions.

KEEP ON GOING: LESSON EXTENSIONS

13. Ask students to imagine being in a segregated school for African American students when they are told that they will now attend a formerly all-White school. Tell students: Write a letter to someone close to you (friend, parent, counselor, brother or sister) expressing your hopes and fears for this new experience.

14. Challenge a partnership, small group of students, or those who choose to wrestle with the issues related to desegregation, using the following scenario: You are on the school board of a segregated school district in May of 1955. Now that the *Brown v. Board of Education* and *Brown II* rulings have been handed down by the Supreme Court, you have been assigned the task of developing a plan for making desegregation peaceful in your school district. Both White parents and Black parents have concerns about the integrated schools. It is summer and the new, integrated school will open in a month. Develop a plan of actions and/or activities for the opening of school that will make things better for all students and their families.

HANDOUT 2.1
PHOTOGRAPHS OF TWO SCHOOLS IN SOUTH CAROLINA, 1950

Liberty Hill Colored School, South Carolina. Reprinted courtesy of South Carolina Department of Archives and History.

White school in Summerton, South Carolina. Courtesy of South Carolina Department of Archives and History.

HANDOUT 2.2
REENACTMENT SCRIPT: *BROWN V. BOARD OF EDUCATION* DECISION

Student Greeter: You may wonder what difference landmark Supreme Court decisions make in our lives today. You might be surprised to find out that students our age have brought cases to the Supreme Court. Did you know that one of the most famous cases in American history—*Brown v. Board of Education*—started with an elementary school girl? Linda Brown was one of the many brave students in the 1950s and 1960s who challenged what was happening around them. She has something to say to us that matters even today.

Linda Brown: Hi, I'm Linda Brown. Even though there was an elementary school close to my house, my sister and I had to go to an all-black school much farther away. We had to get up really early and walk, then take a bus, to the Monroe School in Topeka, Kansas.

We weren't allowed to go to the Sumner School that was closer to us because it was for white children only. Even though some schools in my community were open to everybody, a Kansas law allowed the Board of Education of Topeka to establish segregated elementary schools like the all-white Sumner School in my neighborhood and the all-black Monroe School that I had to attend.

With the help of our lawyer Thurgood Marshall, my family and I sued the Board of Education. Children in other states had the same problem as we did, so when we took our case to the Supreme Court of the United States, the Court combined our cases.

The Court struck down the laws allowing segregated schools. The Justices said that separate is not equal. They ruled that laws segregating students by race were unconstitutional. Today we'll hear from the people whose courage, intelligence, and determination changed history for all of us, starting with Mr. Homer Plessy.

Homer Plessy: My name is Homer Plessy. I was arrested for not giving up my seat to a white man on a train in New Orleans. I decided to challenge my arrest in court. My lawyer argued that separating blacks from whites on the train violated the Fourteenth Amendment. My case made it all of the way to this court. The Court ruled against me in the case of *Plessy v. Ferguson*. The Court said that the states could legally segregate the races, as long as each race was treated "equally." This came to be known as "separate but equal." You can imagine how disappointed I was because for many years courts used my case as an example of supporting segregation.

Charles Hamilton Houston: My name is Charles Hamilton Houston. I was a professor and civil rights lawyer. I saw how segregation between African Americans and whites led to unequal conditions. I made up my mind to establish a record of court victories that showed that separate institutions are NOT equal. This argument was taken up by several of my law students, including Thurgood Marshall and Oliver Hill.

Oliver Hill: My name is Oliver Hill and I was a lawyer. I went to court and won equal pay for black teachers and equal transportation rights for black students. I also won a case that showed the run-down and unequal conditions of schools attended by black students. It was one of the five cases included in the *Brown v. Board of Education* case, which later outlawed segregation in public schools.

Handout 2.2: Reenactment Script: *Brown v. Board of Education* Decision, continued

Constance Baker Motley: My name is Constance Baker Motley. When I was a girl, I wasn't allowed to go to a public skating rink or to the beach because of my race. So I decided to become a civil rights attorney. I worked with Thurgood Marshall on *Brown v. Board of Education*. Some people called me a lion for civil rights. In 1966—about the time some of your parents were born—I became the first African American woman to become a federal judge.

Dr. Kenneth B. Clark: My name is Dr. Kenneth B. Clark. My wife Dr. Mamie Clark and I were psychologists who worked together on what were known as the "doll experiments." They were used by Thurgood Marshall to show that racial segregation sets the stage for African Americans to lose out on equal opportunities.

Dr. Mamie Clark: I am Dr. Mamie Clark. Our work started with my master's degree paper. In our experiments, we had African American children look at a set of white dolls and black dolls. They had to tell us which dolls they liked and wanted to play with. Most African American children chose the white dolls. They described them as better than the black dolls. These experiments showed the terrible impact that racism has—even on children.

Thurgood Marshall: My name is Thurgood Marshall. The first time I saw the Constitution was when I was forced to read it as a punishment for a prank at school. Reading the Constitution was supposed to teach me not to pull pranks. Instead, it inspired me to become a lawyer and fight against discrimination. I went to the Howard University School of Law. After graduation, I worked for the NAACP and successfully argued many cases before the U.S. Supreme Court. *Brown v. Board of Education* was actually five school cases under one name, which showed that separate schools were not equal. Eventually, I became the first African American Justice to serve on the Supreme Court. Today you are going to hear a summary of my argument to the Supreme Court in *Brown v. Board of Education*.

Thurgood Marshall Closing Argument Reader: I got the feeling when I heard the discussion in this court yesterday that when you put a white child in a school with a whole lot of colored children, the white child would fall apart, or something. Everybody knows that is not true. Those same kids in Virginia and South Carolina—and I have seen them do it—they play in the streets together, they play on their farms together, they go down the road together, but they separate to go to school, they come out of school and play ball together. But they have to be separated in school. There must be some magic to it. You can have them voting together, you can have them live in the same neighborhoods. You can have them going to the same state university and the same college, but if they go to elementary and high school together, the world will fall apart.

Chief Justice Earl Warren: My name is Earl Warren. I was the Chief Justice of the United States at the time that the case of *Brown v. Board of Education* was argued. After hearing the case, all nine of us decided that segregation was not legal. Here is a section of the Court's decision, in the words of some eighth graders.

Chief Justice Earl Warren: Opinion Reader: Education is the key to good citizenship. In school, children learn cultural values, prepare for careers, and to be successful in life. It is doubtful that any child can succeed in life if denied education. Education is a right that must be made available to all on equal terms. Separate schools are unequal.

Note. From U.S. Courts (n.d.), *Brown v. Board of Education* re-enactment. Retrieved from http://www.uscourts.gov/educational-resources/get-involved/federal-court-activities/brown-board-education-re-enactment.aspx. Reprinted with permission.

HANDOUT 2.3
THE ROAD TO *BROWN V. BOARD OF EDUCATION*

Key question: Does segregation deprive students of equal protection under the law?

➤ After Reconstruction, the Southern culture maintained the social, economic, and political separation of the races, including separate schools.

➤ In 1865, the 13th Amendment abolished slavery "within the United States, or any place subject to their jurisdiction."

➤ In 1868, the 14th Amendment granted citizenship to all persons "born or naturalized in the United States," including former slaves and provided all citizens with "equal protection under the laws."

➤ The 15th Amendment, ratified in 1870, prohibited states from disenfranchising voters "on account of race, color, or previous condition of servitude."

➤ States could legally institute voter qualifications and they did so by instituting poll taxes, literacy tests, and other qualifications for voting.

➤ States instituted Jim Crow laws between 1876 and 1965. These laws mandated de jure (by law) racial segregation in public facilities including schools in Southern states and de facto (in practice) segregation in Northern states. Conditions for African Americans were inferior to those for White Americans.

➤ The landmark case *Plessy v. Ferguson* (1896) upheld the constitutionality of state laws requiring racial segregation under the doctrine of "separate but equal."

➤ The NAACP organized in 1909 to fight for social justice for all Americans. They began to support the development of African American legal talent to fight segregation.

➤ In the 1930s, the NAACP reported that under segregation, facilities provided for Blacks were always separate but never equal to those for Whites. Thus, the argument supported lawsuits that showed that the "separate but equal" principle had been violated in many cases.

➤ In 1950, the NAACP supported cases that struck down laws requiring segregated graduate schools and the U.S. Supreme Court held that the Equal Protection Clause of the 14th Amendment required the admission of Black students to graduate and professional schools. Other cases were introduced in several states, including education at the elementary and secondary level. All lawyers, parents, and community members who joined this fight against racial injustice did so at their own personal risk and many lost jobs, friends, and even had their homes burned and safety threatened.

➤ In the landmark case *Brown v. Board of Education* (a case in which the Supreme Court combined five separate cases), the NAACP lawyers developed an innovative strategy of using testimony from social scientists and other experts to show that psychological injuries were inflicted on African American school children when segregated. The Supreme Court declared segregation was unconstitutional.

➤ The Brown decision inspired the marches and demonstrations of the Civil Rights Movement of the 1950s and 1960s. These widespread protests ultimately led to the enactment of the Civil Rights Act of 1964, the Voting Rights Act of 1965, and the Fair Housing Act of 1968.

HANDOUT 2.4
1951: *DAVIS ET AL. V. COUNTY SCHOOL BOARD OF PRINCE EDWARD COUNTY, VA*

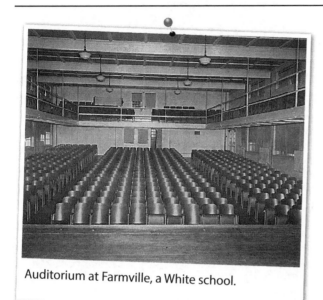

Auditorium at Farmville, a White school.

In 1951, students at Moton High School in Farmville, VA, led by student Barbara Johns, went on strike. They wanted their school board to build them a better school. This high school was typical of the all-Black schools in this central Virginia county. Overcrowded and old, it had no gym, no auditorium, and no cafeteria. Teachers were paid less than those at the all-White high school. Because the efforts of students, the school principal, and the PTA were not met with success, the students decided to strike and asked for help from the NAACP's special counsel for the Southeastern region.

The counsel indicated that the students must sue for the end of segregation if they were to get involved. So the students agreed to challenge segregation, and on May 23, 1951, a lawyer filed suit on behalf of the students and their parents. The suit was filed in the federal district court in Richmond, VA.

This case asked that the state law requiring segregated schools be struck down.

In 1952, the district court decided in favor of the school district and upheld segregation. The case made it to the Supreme Court on appeal. It was heard along with other school segregation cases in Delaware, South Carolina, and Kansas as part of the *Brown v. Board of Education* decision.

OTHER RESOURCES:

➤ http://www.civilrights.org/education/brown/davis.html

➤ http://www.biography.com/people/barbara-johns-206527

Auditorium at Moton, a Black school.

HANDOUT 2.5
1952: *BELTON V. GEBHART* AND *BULAH V. GEBHART*, CLAYMONT AND HOCKESSIN, DE

Ethel Belton and six other adults filed suit on behalf of eight Negro children against Francis B. Gebhart and 12 others (both individuals and state education agencies) in the case *Belton et al. v. Gebhart et al.* The plaintiffs sued the state for denying the children admission to certain public schools because of color or ancestry. The *Belton* case was joined with another very similar Delaware case, *Bulah et al. v. Gebhart et al.* Francis Gebhart, as a member of the State Board of Education of the State of Delaware, was named as the lead defendant in both segregation cases, *Bulah et al. v. Gebhart et al.* and *Belton et al. v. Gebhart et al.*

The Delaware court ruled that these plaintiffs should be admitted to the White schools because they were receiving an inferior education. The court did not, however, decide that "separate but equal" was unlawful. The Board of Education appealed the decision. Both cases were ultimately joined with four other NAACP cases in the Supreme Court ruling in *Brown v. Board of Education.*

OTHER RESOURCES:

➤ http://www.nps.gov/brvb/historyculture/delaware.htm
➤ http://www.civilrights.org/education/brown/belton.html

HANDOUT 2.6
1951: *BRIGGS ET AL. V. ELLIOTT ET AL.*, CLARENDON COUNTY, SC

Twenty African American parents from Clarendon County, SC, sued school officials on behalf of their children in 1950. The schools their children attended were significantly inferior to the White schools in the county. When the NAACP agreed to sponsor a case to seek equal educational opportunities, a local petition for educational equity was the first step. The leader of this effort, Reverend Joseph DeLaine, was fired from his job as a teacher at a local school. Others who signed the petition also lost their jobs, including Mr. and Mrs. Briggs. To support their families, Reverend DeLaine and Mr. Briggs moved to other states.

The NAACP asked Thurgood Marshall to participate in this case at the state level, challenging segregation, arguing that segregation itself harmed their children, as they suffered psychological harm in a segregated environment. The lawyers introduced evidence from social scientists showing how segregation harmed Black school children. This went beyond the argument that school buildings were inferior. The United States District Court ruled that the schools attended by African American children were inferior to the White schools, and they ordered the school system to equalize the facilities. But, because the children were denied admission to White schools during the period of school upgrading, the case was appealed to the United States Supreme Court. The case was one of five separate cases heard concurrently by the United States Supreme Court under the collective title *Brown v. Board of Education*.

OTHER RESOURCES:

➤ http://www.civilrights.org/education/brown/briggs.html
➤ http://www.nps.gov/brvb/historyculture/socarolina.htm

HANDOUT 2.7
1950: *BOLLING V. SHARPE,* WASHINGTON, DC

In Washington, DC, several students, including 12-year-old Spottswood Bolling, were denied admission to the far superior White public schools. This denial was solely because of their race or color.

The case was dismissed by the U.S. District Court. The Supreme Court asked to review this case in conjunction with *Brown v. Board of Education* combined cases. The Supreme Court would eventually file a separate opinion on *Bolling* because the 14th Amendment was not applicable in Washington, DC.

OTHER RESOURCES:

➤ http://www.nps.gov/brvb/historyculture/districtofcolumbia.htm
➤ http://www.oyez.org/cases/1950-1959/1952/1952_8

HANDOUT 2.8
1951: *BROWN V. BOARD OF EDUCATION*, TOPEKA, KS

Linda Brown was a third-grade student in Topeka, KS, whose father wanted her to go a White school just seven blocks from her home. She currently had to walk six blocks, passing through a railroad switchyard, and then board a bus to reach her Black elementary school. Her father agreed to join with the NAACP to challenge segregation in the Topeka schools, joining with other plaintiffs who tried unsuccessfully to enroll their children in White schools. Brown was chosen as the lead plaintiff before the District Court. The Court ruled in favor of the Board of Education in Topeka. A three-judge panel at the U.S. District Court in Topeka unanimously held that "no willful, intentional or substantial discrimination" existed in Topeka's schools. The NAACP appealed to the U.S. Supreme Court, where the Brown case was combined with four other cases challenging school segregation in other places including Virginia, South Carolina, Delaware, and Washington, DC.

The decision was appealed and became part of the groundbreaking *Brown* v. *Board of Education* decision.

OTHER RESOURCES:

➤ http://www.streetlaw.org/en/landmark/cases/brown_v_board_of_education
➤ http://brownvboard.org/
➤ http://www.nps.gov/brvb/historyculture/kansas.htm

HANDOUT 2.9
NOTES ON *BROWN V. BOARD OF EDUCATION* COURT CASES

	Location	Complaint	Issues	Ruling
Brown v. Board of Education	Topeka, KS			
Bolling v. Sharpe	Washington, DC			
Bulah v. Gebhart and *Belton v. Gebhart*	Delaware			
Davis v. School Board of Prince Edward County	Prince Edward County, VA			
Briggs v. Elliott	Clarendon County, SC			

HANDOUT 2.10
BROWN V. BOARD OF EDUCATION
MAJORITY OPINION EXCERPTS

The decision was unanimous. Chief Justice Earl Warren delivered the majority opinion:

. . . there are findings below that the Negro and white schools involved have been equalized, or are being equalized, with respect to buildings, curricula, qualifications and salaries of teachers, and other "tangible" factors. Our decision, therefore, cannot turn on merely a comparison of these tangible factors in the Negro and white schools involved in each of the cases. We must look instead to the effect of segregation itself on public education . . .

We must consider public education in the light of its full development and its present place in American life throughout the Nation. Only in this way can it be determined if segregation in public schools deprives these plaintiffs of the equal protection of the laws . . .

Today, education is perhaps the most important function of state and local governments. Compulsory school attendance laws and the great expenditures for education both demonstrate our recognition of the importance of education to our democratic society. It is required in the performance of our most basic public responsibilities, even service in the armed forces. It is the very foundation of good citizenship. Today it is a principal instrument in awakening the child to cultural values, in preparing him for later professional training, and in helping him to adjust normally to his environment. In these days, it is doubtful that any child may reasonably be expected to succeed in life if he is denied the opportunity of an education. Such an opportunity, where the state has undertaken to provide it, is a right which must be made available to all on equal terms.

We come then to the question presented: Does segregation of children in public schools solely on the basis of race, even though the physical facilities and other "tangible" factors may be equal, deprive the children of the minority group of equal educational opportunities? We believe that it does.

We conclude that, in the field of public education, the doctrine of "separate but equal" has no place. Separate educational facilities are inherently unequal. Therefore, we hold that the plaintiffs and others similarly situated for whom the actions have been brought are, by reason of the segregation complained of, deprived of the equal protection of the laws guaranteed by the Fourteenth Amendment.

HANDOUT 2.11
BROWN II MAJORITY OPINION EXCERPTS

The decision was unanimous. Chief Justice Earl Warren delivered the majority opinion:

Racial discrimination in public education is unconstitutional, 347 U.S. 483, 497, and all provisions of federal, state or local law requiring or permitting such discrimination must yield to this principle.

The judgments below (except that in the Delaware case) are reversed and the cases are remanded to the District Courts to take such proceedings and enter such orders and decrees consistent with this opinion as are necessary and proper to admit the parties to these cases to public schools on a racially nondiscriminatory basis with all deliberate speed.

School authorities have the primary responsibility for elucidating, assessing and solving the varied local school problems which may require solution in fully implementing the governing constitutional principles.

Courts will have to consider whether the action of school authorities constitutes good faith implementation of the governing constitutional principles

At stake is the personal interest of the plaintiffs in admission to public schools as soon as practicable on a nondiscriminatory basis.

Courts of equity may properly take into account the public interest in the elimination in a systematic and effective manner of a variety of obstacles in making the transition to school systems operated in accordance with the constitutional principles . . . but the vitality of these constitutional principles cannot be allowed to yield simply because of disagreement with them.

While giving weight to these public and private considerations, the courts will require that the defendants make a prompt and reasonable start toward full compliance with the ruling of this Court.

Once such a start has been made, the courts may find that additional time is necessary to carry out the ruling in an effective manner.

The burden rests on the defendants to establish that additional time is necessary in the public interest and is consistent with good faith compliance at the earliest practicable date.

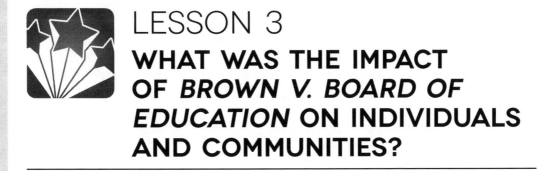

LESSON 3
WHAT WAS THE IMPACT OF *BROWN V. BOARD OF EDUCATION* ON INDIVIDUALS AND COMMUNITIES?

OVERVIEW

LESSON AT A GLANCE

> Students read and listen to interviews of people who experienced the desegregation of public schools.

> Students examine the process of preparing for an oral history, interviewing selected people, and recording the oral history for an audience (using video, audio tape, or written notes).

TIMELINE EVENTS

> 1954: Supreme Court declares separate schools are unequal

> 1955: Supreme Court orders lower federal courts to use "all deliberate speed"

> 1956: Southern states resist school desegregation

> 1956: Virginia supports "massive resistance"

> 1957: Little Rock, AR, requires National Guard to protect nine Black students integrating the high school

> 1958: March on Washington by 10,000 youth in support of integration

> 1959: March on Washington with 25,000 participants

> 1959: Prince Edward County, VA, closes public schools

> 1963: Supreme Court orders Prince Edward County to integrate its schools

ESSENTIAL QUESTIONS

> How do historians acquire accurate information about the experiences of people from long ago?

> What was the personal and social impact of school desegregation on students who experienced it?

> How do court decisions become part of everyday life in the United States?

> How were the goals of the NAACP met?

> How did the *Brown v. Board of Education* decision impact the Civil Rights Movement?

CONCEPTUAL UNDERSTANDINGS

➤ The *Brown v. Board of Education* decision was a landmark decision, ending legal segregation in public schools in the United States.

➤ The Supreme Court decision overruled *Plessy v. Ferguson* and declared that racially segregated facilities are inherently unequal and have a detrimental effect on both Blacks and Whites.

➤ Forced desegregation of schools served as a catalyst for the Civil Rights Movement.

➤ The Civil Rights Movement was a purposeful quest for racial equality that began with grassroots efforts.

➤ A cultural shift in America occurred because of the effects of the Civil Rights Movement.

IMPORTANT TERMS AND IDEAS

➤ *overrule*: to rule against

➤ *catalyst*: person or thing that causes a change or event

➤ *detrimental*: causing damage

➤ *desegregation*: the process of removing the separation of the races

➤ *oral history*: collecting, preserving, and interpreting the voices and memories of people

➤ *"colored"*: offensive term for those who are not White, used in the past in particular for African Americans

➤ *integration*: the combining of races, especially in schools and public places

➤ *massive resistance*: large scale actions to avoid some legal requirement

➤ *perspective*: one's mental view of something

MATERIALS

➤ Video clips of oral histories (see suggested resources)

➤ Handout 3.1: Where Did States Stand on School Segregation?

➤ Handout 3.2: Educational Separation in the U.S. Prior to *Brown v. Board of Education*

➤ Handout 3.3: Analyzing a Situation

SUGGESTED RESOURCES

➤ Morrison, T. (2004). *Remember: The journey to school integration*. New York, NY: Houghton Mifflin.

➤ Thomas, J. C. (2003). *Linda Brown, you are not alone: The Brown v. Board of Education decision*. New York, NY: Hyperion Books for Children.

➤ http://www.npr.org/templates/story/story.php?storyid=1853532

➤ http://www.loc.gov/exhibits/brown

➤ http://americanhistory.si.edu/brown/history/

➤ http://americanhistory.si.edu/brown/resources/electronic-field-trips.html

➤ http://www.folklife.si.edu/education_exhibits/resources/guide/introduction.aspx

INSTRUCTIONS

THE HOOK

1. Distribute Handout 3.1: Where Did States Stand on School Segregation? Ask students to work with a partner to shade in the states that they believe would have required segregation before the Supreme Court's *Brown v. Brown of Education* decision. Which states might have banned segregation?

2. Allow a few minutes for students to complete their maps and then display Handout 3.2: Educational Separation in the U.S. Prior to *Brown v. Board of Education*. Tell them that there were 17 states that required segregation in public schools: Alabama, Arkansas, Delaware, Florida, Georgia, Kentucky, Louisiana, Maryland, Mississippi, Missouri, North Carolina, Oklahoma, South Carolina, Tennessee, Texas, Virginia, and West Virginia. Four others permitted school segregation: Arizona, Kansas, New Mexico, and Wyoming. Ask students to put a check at the location of each of the five locations involved in *Brown v. Board of Education* (Topeka, KS; Summerton, SC; Farmville, VA; Washington, DC; and Wilmington, DE). One of the Supreme Court Justices stated: "We consolidated them and made Brown the first so that the whole question would not smack of being a purely Southern one." What do you think he meant by this statement?

DEVELOPING CONCEPTUAL UNDERSTANDING

3. Ask students if they have ever been interviewed. Why are people likely to be interviewed? What if you could interview a person who actually experienced school segregation? What do you think you would learn? In what ways would it be different from reading a news story? Tell students you just happen to have a video clip of an interview with a person who had this experience. Select a section from an interview with a person who experienced segregation in school. You may choose a video clip, an audio piece, or a transcript. One suggested source is "Oral Histories From Segregated Evansville, Indiana in the 1960s" (https://www.youtube.com/watch?v=5vTYyLqvYVQ).

4. Ask students to listen to the interview and note any issues they hear that might be related to the *Brown v. Board of Education* Supreme Court decision. After the interview, ask students to make connections to the court case, reminding students that the decision of the court required desegregation to occur "with all deliberate speed." Ask them to imagine being a student, a teacher, a principal, or a parent, and consider what they might anticipate if they were to soon experience desegregation. Would this occur differently in the North than in the South? Why?

5. Tell students that the interview they just heard was an example of oral history and let them know that in this lesson they will work in small groups to examine other oral histories. Tell students: *Oral histories often help us to picture what things were really like long ago. For example some of you read about the trouble in Prince Edward County, VA, in the early 1950s. Which group learned about this in our last lesson? What happened in Prince Edward County as a result of* Brown v. Board of Education*?*

6. Ask this group to share their response. Fill in any gaps. Tell students that in the state of Virginia there was a call for "Massive Resistance" to integration. This was a group of laws

passed in the state in 1958 so that schools could avoid complying with the order for desegregation. These included grants for tuition to students who opposed integration, power for Pupil Placement Boards to assign students to specific schools, and a law that cut off state funds and closed any public school that agreed to integrate.

Teacher's Note. As part of Virginia's Massive Resistance campaign, the Prince Edward County schools refused to integrate, choosing instead to pay for White students to attend private schools. In 1959, when the state stopped funding the White private schools, the Prince Edward County Board of Supervisors refused to give any funding to the public schools, effectively closing them down completely. The public schools remained closed for 5 years.

7. Tell students you are going to show them a brief (about 2.5 minute) video clip from an interview with Calvin Nunnally, a student in Prince Edward County schools at the time of the school closing (http://www2.vcdh.virginia.edu/reHIST604/cnvideo.html). Ask students to record two things they hear in the interview that they believe are examples of unfair treatment and to think about the kinds of questions the interviewer asked Mr. Nunnally.

8. Show the clip from the beginning up until Mr. Nunnally speaks about going to college. After viewing the clip, show students the transcript of the interview available at the same website, using a digital projector. Say:
   a. The video clip you just saw was an edited version of the whole interview.
   b. Can you remember one of the questions the interviewer asked?
   c. Which questions are open-ended (show transcript) and which are specific (names, dates, particular details)?

   You may want to point out the place in the transcript where the interviewer asks Mr. Nunnally to use complete sentences in response to questions. Ask why he might have done this? Tell students that the goal is to get an accurate recording of what happened, so the details in relation to the question are more important than a polished interview.

9. Ask students who else in Prince Edward County might be a good person to interview for an oral history about this topic. List ideas on the board. Talk about how having multiple perspectives could provide a fuller picture of what was happening at the time and place in history. Project a copy of Handout 3.3: Analyzing a Situation and ask students to assist you in completing the organizer based on Mr. Nunnally's story.

10. Tell students: *Today you will have an opportunity to listen to another interview (or watch or read a transcript) of someone who has a story to tell about school integration. It will be important for you to analyze the comments of the person being interviewed and think about what you learn related to school integration. After your group has viewed or listened to the interview, work with a partner to complete notes. You will be responding to these questions as you complete this task:*
    a. What information did you receive?

    b.   Who was involved in the situation? When?

    c.   What were the different points of view presented at the time?

    d.   What ideas do we need to understand?

    e.   What questions are you left with?

When your group members are finished, share your thoughts about the interview with each other.

11.   Assign students to oral history teams (4–6 students) to listen to and/or read transcripts of interviews of people telling stories related to school integration at different times and places in history. You may assign more than one group to the same interview. Distribute copies of 3.3: Analyzing a Situation to students for use in this activity.

    a.   Interview One: Melba Pattillo: Little Rock, AR
- Video: http://www.pbslearningmedia.org/resource/iml04.soc.ush.civil.beals/melba-pattillo-beals/
- Transcript: http://d43fweuh3sg51.cloudfront.net/media/assets/wgbh/iml04/iml04_doc_fullbeals/iml04_doc_fullbeals.pdf

    b.   Interview Two: Ruby Bridges: New Orleans, LA
- Audio: http://cpa.ds.npr.org/wwno/audio/2012/12/Sharon_RubySecond.mp3

    c.   Interview Three: Carl Eggleston: Prince Edward County, VA
- Transcript: http://www2.vcdh.virginia.edu/saxon/servlet/SaxonServlet?source=/xml_docs/modernva/modernva_transcripts.xml&style=/xml_docs/modernva/interview_modernva.xsl&level=single&id=Carl_Eggleston

    d.   Interview Four: Fran Jackson, North Carolina
- Audio and transcript: http://docsouth.unc.edu/sohp/K-0208/menu.html

12.   Ask students: *In what ways did the people in your interviews experience school segregation? Allow time for each group to present a summary of their interview and findings. Then say: Let's hear from each group and think about connections we can make across these interviews. After groups share their interviews, ask the class for words or phrases to express the experiences and related feelings of people who experienced school segregation. Record their ideas on a two-column chart (Experience/Feelings). Conclude by asking students in what ways interviews might be a good source of data for a historian.*

SOAR: SUMMARIZE, OBSERVE, ASSESS, REFLECT:

13.   *Do you think there are still people alive who remember the Civil Rights Movement? Might there be people in our community? Talk with your partner and think about where you might find someone to interview. Discuss the interview process. What makes a good interview? How would you prepare for an interview? What types of questions work best?*

THINK AGAIN: HOMEWORK

14. After students have discussed possibilities for people to interview, tell them that for homework they should continue to think about possible people to interview and also to develop three questions that might be used in an interview about segregation in the 1950s and 1960s.

KEEP ON GOING: LESSON EXTENSIONS

15. From the list of possible interviewees, select one or two to invite to class to discuss their experiences during the time of the Civil Rights Movement. Ask selected students or volunteers to prepare for the visitor(s), selecting the questions and format for the interview and preparing for the recording of the event. Alternatively, ask a small group of students to prepare for and facilitate a private interview, reporting on their findings to the whole class.

16. Challenge students (entire class or selected students) to locate oral history interviews from other groups who experienced discrimination in their schooling or community life at some time in U.S. history (American Indians, Japanese internment victims, immigrants) and create a collection for the class to use.

Teacher's Note. The option for the entire class to complete oral histories as a unit project is described in the unit introduction.

HANDOUT 3.1
WHERE DID STATES STAND ON SCHOOL SEGREGATION?

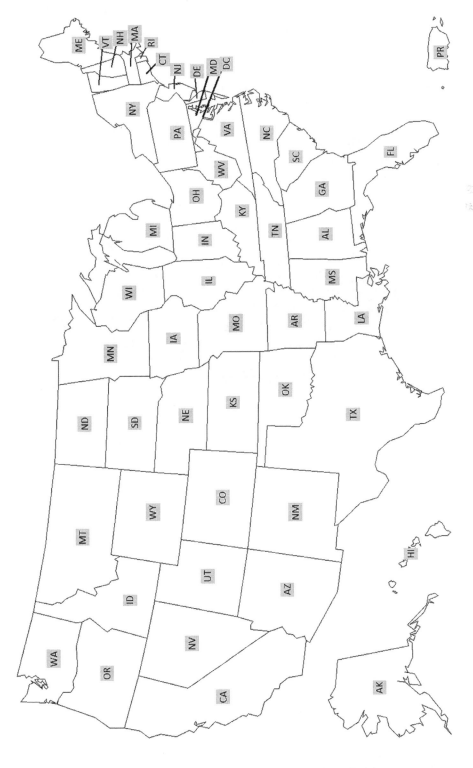

HANDOUT 3.2
EDUCATIONAL SEPARATION IN THE U.S. PRIOR TO *BROWN V. BOARD OF EDUCATION*

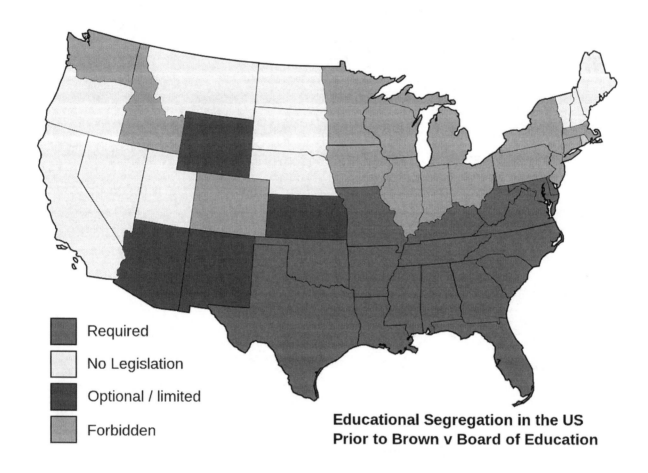

Required

No Legislation

Optional / limited

Forbidden

Educational Segregation in the US Prior to Brown v Board of Education

NAME:_____ DATE:_____

 HANDOUT 3.3
ANALYZING A SITUATION

The Issue

The Important Information

The Time Period

Person/Group	Point of View

The Concepts We Need to Understand

Questions

LESSON 4
WAS *BROWN V. BOARD OF EDUCATION* SUCCESSFUL?

OVERVIEW

LESSON AT A GLANCE

➤ Students participate in a Structured Academic Controversy focused on the key question, "Was *Brown v. Board of Education* successful?"

➤ Students consider both sides of the controversy, analyzing both the short-term and long-term effects of the court decision.

TIMELINE EVENTS

➤ 1954: Supreme Court rules on landmark *Brown v. Board of Education* case

➤ 1955: Supreme Court directs states to move "with all deliberate speed"

ESSENTIAL QUESTIONS

➤ In what ways was desegregation aided by the *Brown v. Board of Education* decision?

➤ What are the short- and long-term effects of *Brown v. Board of Education*?

CONCEPTUAL UNDERSTANDINGS

➤ Supreme Court decisions are not always unanimous. The decision in *Brown v. Board of Education* was unanimous.

➤ Equality may be ordered by law but implementation requires cultural, social, and economic changes.

➤ The quest for equality for all citizens continues to the present day.

IMPORTANT TERMS AND IDEAS

➤ *unanimous*: all in complete agreement

➤ *consensus*: coming to general agreement

➤ *clarify*: to remove confusion

➤ *controversy*: dispute, debate, argument, often of long standing

➤ *prosecutor*: public officer charged with representing the prosecution

MATERIALS

➤ Handout 4.1: What Happened After *Brown v. Board of Education*?
➤ Handout 4.2: Round One: "Yes, *Brown v. Board of Education* Was Successful"
➤ Handout 4.3: Round One: "No, *Brown v. Board of Education* Was Not Successful"
➤ Handout 4.4: Round Two: "Yes, *Brown v. Board of Education* Was Successful"
➤ Handout 4.5: Round Two: "No, *Brown v. Board of Education* Was Not Successful"

SUGGESTED RESOURCES

➤ Ogletree, C. (2005). *All deliberate speed: Reflections on the first half-century of Brown v. Board of Education*. New York, NY: Norton & Co.
➤ http://www.ourdocuments.gov/doc.php?flash=true&doc=87&page=transcript
➤ http://www.americanbar.org/content/dam/aba/migrated/brown/brownvboard. authcheckdam.pdf
➤ http://civilrightsproject.ucla.edu/research/k-12-education/integration-and-diversity/ brown-at-50-king2019s-dream-or-plessy2019s-nightmare/?searchterm=brown%20 at%2050
➤ http://civilrightsproject.ucla.edu/research/k-12-education/integration-and-diversity/ brown-at-60-great-progress-a-long-retreat-and-an-uncertain-future

INSTRUCTIONS

THE HOOK

1. Distribute copies of Handout 4.1: What Happened After *Brown v. Board of Education*? Ask students to work in small groups to categorize these events in some way. Tell groups they have just 5 minutes to think up categories and code the events according to their categorizations. Then ask groups to share how they made their categories and discuss why certain events fit the category. If you wish, you may provide students with categories (by state, by action, by groups of people, etc.) and then ask groups to code events by these categories.

Teacher's Note. Students will work in groups of four for the Structured Academic Controversy reading and discussion. Prior to class, arrange desks in fours and assign students to fairly similar ability groups. Partners will sit on the same side, with opposing partners facing them. You may place nametags on the desks or post a seating chart. Although groups of four are ideal, you may require one or two larger groups to accommodate your class size.

DEVELOPING CONCEPTUAL UNDERSTANDING

2. Tell students: *Just imagine. It is 1954. You are a member of the Supreme Court. You and your fellow judges have just reached a unanimous decision in the* Brown v. Board of Education *case. You have overturned* Plessy v. Ferguson, *in which the court stated that segregation was legal and constitutional as long as "facilities were equal." What is one reason you had for deciding, as a judge, that separate is really not equal? Think about this for a minute and then turn to your partner and decide on one reason you would have decided that separate facilities are not equal facilities.*

3. Ask several partners for their ideas and ask the class if others came to the same conclusion.

4. Tell students that in this lesson they are going to examine the consequences of the *Brown v. Board of Education* decision to decide whether or not this decision was a success. Let them know that they will read and discuss this issue using a Structured Academic Controversy (SAC) method. They will work with a partner to share ideas on both sides of the question "Was *Brown v. Board of Education* a success?"

5. Tell students: *A Structured Academic Controversy will help you to understand differing points of view related to the* Brown v. Board of Education *decision. You are trying to decide if the decision was successful ("Yes") or not successful ("No"). The SAC will have two rounds of discussion. You and your partner will first read and present one side of the issue in round one and then, in round two, you will read and present the opposite side of the controversy. I will give you new information to review with your partner for each round. You will have a chance to be persuasive for each side—yes,* Brown v. Board of Education *was successful and no,* Brown v. Board of Education *was not successful. This is an academic controversy because there are legitimate opposing viewpoints on the question that each side has at least some evidence to support. In round two, you must prepare and present the opposite point of view from your first round.*

6. Ask students what they think will be challenging about this form of discussion.

7. Seat students in groups of four, with opposite sides facing each other. Assign two students to begin the "yes, it was successful" analysis and discussion and the other two students to begin the "no" side of the analysis and discussion. It is helpful for keeping track of sides to keep all "yes" pairs facing one side of the room and all "no" pairs facing the other side of the room.

8. Provide students with the appropriate "yes" or "no" information sheets (Handouts 4.2 and 4.3) and direct them to read the paper and prepare to offer their best reasons why their position is the correct one. Instruct students to read through the article for their position and identify and discuss which points they believe are the strongest. These are the ones they should focus on during their presentation. They should decide which partner is going to present which arguments. Each member must participate. Allow about 5 minutes for the students to prepare their ideas.

9. Review the SAC process with students by saying: *This is called a structured discussion because it is not a wide open debate but a chance to practice persuading each other to believe in the side of the issue that you will be representing.* Help students differentiate between a discussion and a debate, explaining that controversy means there is an academic disagreement about the issue. It is not a situation where people are angry. The goal is to better understand the issue from different perspectives and to determine whether or not there are any areas where they can build consensus, meaning that they find agreement.

10. **Round one.** Students present their arguments to the opposing side. The "for" or concurring arguments ("yes") will go first, followed by clarifying questions, and then the "anti" or dissenting arguments ("no") will present and receive questions. Each side will have the opportunity to present for 3 minutes (may need to adjust this), followed by one minute for clarifying questions. Emphasize that clarifying questions should be directed at increasing understanding of what the opponent said, not at enhancing one's own argument or arguing against what the opponent said. You will need to watch the time and judge how quickly students are able to present sides. It is okay for them to feel a little rushed, as it will keep up the tempo of the lesson. Remind them that they will hear about each side twice through the two rounds.

Teacher's Note. Model the concept of clarifying questions before starting round one of the presentations (Were you saying that . . . ? Can you explain what you mean by . . . ? Can you share a little more about that?). This is not a debate opportunity, but a chance to ask the other side to clarify something or provide more information about something they said. Remind students that they will be working on effective discussion skills, including good posture, looking the opposing side in the eyes, and keeping their feet on the floor. If students are resistant to arguing a side they do not agree with or arguing both sides, remind them that they will be able to share their personal views on the issue at the end.

11. **Round two: Reverse positions.** The partnerships will switch positions and receive new data sheets (Handouts 4.4 and 4.5). This time, when students look at the arguments, they may present any arguments they wish, but should be encouraged to consider the ones the first presenters did not use. Again, partners should determine who will argue which point. Presentations will proceed exactly as before. The "for"/"yes" arguments will speak for 3 minutes, followed by clarifying questions for one minute, and ending with the "anti"/"no" side's presentation and clarifying questions.

12. **Group discussion/Attempts to reach consensus.** Following the second presentation of positions, the students should discuss (within their small group) their reactions and personal opinions. Instruct groups to choose a recorder (or choose one for them) to write down the group consensus. If any group members cannot agree, they may write their own "minority opinion" just as in Supreme Court decisions. These opinion statements should be attached to the group statement. Encourage groups to come to consensus based on the evidence in front of them. They may be able to agree on at least some aspects of the issue.

SOAR: SUMMARIZE, OBSERVE, ASSESS, REFLECT

13. At the end of the consensus discussion, ask groups to share their thoughts with the class. Debrief on the overall discussion and ask students to share a plus, minus, and interesting thought (PMI) about participating in a Structured Academic Controversy. Offer the class

your feedback on the process and their contributions to the analysis of this very important Supreme Court decision.

THINK AGAIN: HOMEWORK

14. Ask students to again imagine themselves as one of the judges in the *Brown v. Board of Education* case. Direct them to write a letter to a class of African American middle school students describing their hopes for changes the students might see in their educational opportunities in the future, remembering that this is 1954.

KEEP ON GOING: LESSON EXTENSIONS

15. Invite students who may need or desire additional challenges to locate news stories reporting on the *Brown v. Board of Education* decision, using the following resources or others they are able to locate. A quick Internet search can begin by using the terms "Brown v. Board newspaper article" and looking under images. Two additional sites are: http://cjonline.com/indepth/brown/archives/ and http://www.nytimes.com/learning/general/onthisday/990517onthisday_big.html. Ask students to create a brief editorial or letter to the editor that might have appeared in their city's newspaper that day.

HANDOUT 4.1
WHAT HAPPENED AFTER *BROWN V. BOARD OF EDUCATION?*

1954	In *Brown v. Board of Education*, the Supreme Court rules that racial segregation in public schools violates the 14th Amendment. This decision overturns the "separate but equal" doctrine that enabled segregation.
1955	In the decision in *Brown II*, the Supreme Court orders the lower courts to require desegregation "with all deliberate speed."
1956	The first African American student is enrolled at the University of Alabama. Riots occur and the student is expelled for criticizing the school. The state of Virginia calls for "massive resistance" and promises to close schools rather than desegregate.
1957	Nine Black students are escorted to Central High School in Little Rock, AR, by National Guard troops.
1958	The NAACP wins a Supreme Court ruling barring the Governor of Arkansas from interfering with integration in Little Rock.
1959	Prince Edward County, VA, closes its public schools. 25,000 youth march in Washington, DC, in support of integration.
1960	Ruby Bridges is protected by federal marshals in New Orleans as she enrolls in school.
1962	The University of Mississippi admits its first African American student, James Meredith, and more than 2,000 Whites riot.
1963	Two African American students register at the University of Alabama after President Kennedy federalizes the Alabama National Guard.
1964	The Civil Rights Act is passed by Congress. It bans discrimination in schools, public facilities, voting, and employment. Prince Edward County is ordered to reopen its schools.
1965	Rev. Martin Luther King leads a 5-day march for voting rights from Selma, AL, to Montgomery, AL. Congress passes the Voting Rights Act.
1967	Thurgood Marshall becomes the first African American Supreme Court Justice.
1969	The Supreme Court orders Mississippi schools desegregated immediately.
1971	The Supreme Court upholds busing, magnet schools, compensatory education, and other remedies to facilitate desegregation of public schools.

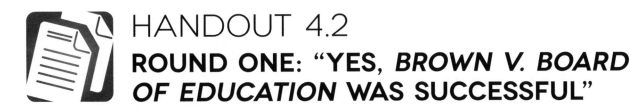

HANDOUT 4.2
ROUND ONE: "YES, *BROWN V. BOARD OF EDUCATION* WAS SUCCESSFUL"

AMERICANS FAVOR DESEGREGATION

". . . an overwhelming majority of Americans favor desegregated schools. Likewise, almost all parents want their children to be prepared to get along with children of all backgrounds in a society that is on pace to become half non-White within their lifetimes.

According to a recent Gallup Poll, increasing majorities of Americans believe that integration has improved the quality of education for both Blacks and Whites. This does not mean that most Americans do not also prefer neighborhood schools—they do—but it makes clear that most people would like integrated schools if they didn't have to do anything in order to get them." (Southern Poverty Law Center, 2013, para. 4–5)

TABLE 1
Percent of Black Students in Majority White Schools in the South, 1954–2001

Year	Percent Black in Majority White Schools
1954	0
1960	.1
1964	2.3
1967	13.9
1968	23.4
1970	33.1
1972	36.4
1976	37.6
1980	37.1
1986	42.9
1988	43.5
1991	39.2
1994	36.6
1996	34.7
1998	32.7
2000	31.0
2001	30.2

Note. From *Brown at 50: King's dream or Plessy's nightmare?* by G. Orfield & C. Lee (p. 19), 2004, Cambridge, MA: Harvard University, The Civil Rights Project. Copyright 2004 The Civil Rights Project. Retrieved from http://civilrightsproject.ucla.edu/research/k-12-education/integration-and-diversity/brown-at-50-king2019s-dream-or-plessy2019s-nightmare/orfield-brown-50-2004.pdf

Handout 4.2: Round One: "Yes, *Brown v. Board of Education* Was Successful", continued

NARROWING OF EDUCATIONAL ACHIEVEMENT GAP

"From the early 1970s until the late 1980s, a very large narrowing of the achievement gap (between Black and White students) occurred in both reading and mathematics. For some cohorts the gaps were cut by as much as half or more. In reading, for example, a 39-point gap for 13-year-olds in 1971 was reduced to an 18-point gap in 1988. For 17-year-olds, the gap declined from 53 points to 20 points. In mathematics, the gaps also were narrowed significantly." (Barton & Coley, 2010, p. 6)

END OF LEGALIZED SEGREGATED SOCIETY

"Brown was a success in getting rid of a racial caste system. . . . The chief victory is that average Americans everywhere now embrace the view that America should be a free, open, integrationist society where no one is limited in their access to education or jobs or whatever, based on their race."—Sheryll Cashin, in a 2004 interview with PBS *NewsHour*'s Gwen Ifill

BETTER INTERRACIAL RELATIONSHIPS

Studies have shown long-term social benefits from integrated schools. Students who have attended racially integrated schools exhibit fewer racial stereotypes and greater cross-racial understanding. The younger students are when they attend integrated schools the more likely they are to exhibit positive interracial relationship. Students who attend diverse schools are also more likely to attend integrated colleges, work in environments with diverse populations, and live in integrated communities. These findings are true for both African American and white students (Tefera, Frankenberg, Siegel-Hawley, & Chirichigno, 2011).

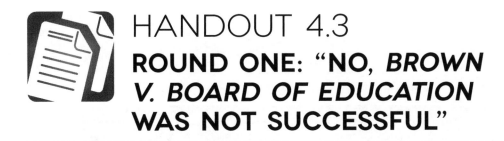

HANDOUT 4.3
ROUND ONE: "NO, *BROWN V. BOARD OF EDUCATION* WAS NOT SUCCESSFUL"

LOSS OF BLACK TEACHERS

More than 38,000 Black educators in 17 states lost their jobs between 1954 and 1965, some due to school closings and student/faculty integration. This in part has led to a great shortage in Black teachers today.

Students who need effective teachers the most—low income and minority students—are far less likely to have qualified and experienced teachers than White students and students in more affluent districts.

- ➤ High-poverty schools have a 50% higher rate of low-scoring teachers (bottom quartile SAT/ACT scores; Education Week, 2001).
- ➤ The percentage of teachers in high poverty districts without full certification is almost double the percentage for all other districts (U.S. Department of Education, 2011).

In order to fill shortages of qualified teachers, programs such as Teach for America have been developed. The ratio of Teach for America teachers identifying as people of color is more than double that of teachers nationwide (Teach for America, 2012).

"WHITE FLIGHT"

"Throughout the country, patterns of housing and immigration have created neighborhoods that are extremely segregated. And in such areas, the quality of education provided by public schools is far from equal. Nowhere is this more evident than in California, where 100 percent of the students in some schools are members of minority groups." (Sanchez & Jaffe, 2004, para. 2)

"Today our public schools are more segregated than they were in 1970, before the Supreme Court ordered busing and other measures to achieve desegregation" (Southern Poverty Law Center, 2013, para. 13).

"BRIGHT FLIGHT"

"For schools that had long served black students during segregation, the *Brown* decision allowed the best teachers and most motivated students to seek better opportunities elsewhere. It's a familiar scene in America's inner cities: All-black schools that were pillars of excellence under segregation have now become painful victims of 'bright flight.'" (Norris, 2004, para. 2)

School choice programs and charter schools, intended to help students gain the best education available, have also created "bright flight." These programs, which attempt to provide quality education through providing choice of schools, often result in high achieving students leaving urban public schools for private, charter, or suburban schools.

Handout 4.3: Round One: "No, *Brown v. Board of Education* Was Not Successful", continued

TABLE 2
Student Segregation by Race/Ethnicity, 1988–1989

	% of Students in 50–100% Minority Schools	% of Students in 90–100% Minority Schools	% of White Students in School of Average Student
White	7.9	0.4	83.4
Black	64.6	33.5	35.2
Latino	71.8	33.4	32.3
Asian	50.9	12.9	49.0
Am. Indian	377.0	17.8	55.7

Note. From "Reviving the Goal of an Integrated Society: A 21st Century Challenge" (p. 13) by Gary Orfield, 2009, UCLA Civil Rights Project. Retrieved from http://civilrightsproject.ucla.edu/research/k-12-education/integration-and-diversity/reviving-the-goal-of-an-integrated-society-a-21st-century-challenge/?searchterm=reviving%20the%20goal. Reprinted with permission.

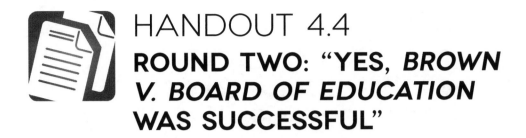

HANDOUT 4.4
ROUND TWO: "YES, *BROWN V. BOARD OF EDUCATION* WAS SUCCESSFUL"

DESEGREGATION LEADS TO INCREASED EARNINGS AND SCHOOL COMPLETION RATES

The earnings gap between Southern-born Black men and non-Southern-born Black men narrowed by about 10% after desegregation, the National Bureau of Economic Research reported in 2005. Some of this positive change may have been because of the general allocation of better resources to all schools even prior to desegregation. The authors of this report (Ashenfelter, Collins, and Yoon) argued that better schools and school desegregation tended to raise the earnings of Southern-born Black men.

Starting in the mid-1960s, school desegregation in the South proceeded rapidly as a combined result of the Civil Rights Act of 1964, the Elementary and Secondary Education Act of 1965, and a series of federal court orders. The NBER researchers found desegregation was consistent with a positive and economically significant effect on the income and high school completion rates of Black students.

DESEGREGATION HAS "SUBSTANTIAL BENEFITS"

"Desegregation progress was very substantial for blacks, and occurred in the South from the mid-1960s to the late 1980s. Contrary to many claims, the South has not gone back to the level of segregation before Brown. It has lost all of the additional progress made after 1967 but is still the least segregated region for black students . . . .

A half century of research shows that many forms of unequal opportunity are linked to segregation. Further, research also finds that desegregated education has substantial benefits for educational and later life outcomes for students from all backgrounds." (Orfield et al., 2014, para. 3, 8).

HANDOUT 4.5
ROUND TWO: "NO, *BROWN V. BOARD OF EDUCATION* WAS NOT SUCCESSFUL"

CHANGING SCHOOLS

Even before the *Brown v. Board of Education* decision, changes were occurring in schools in the South. For example, as David Francis noted in a summary of a National Bureau of Economic Research report, in Alabama in 1910, the average school year for White students was more than 30 days longer than for Blacks. In classrooms, there were about 12 more Black students per teacher than White students per teacher. These conditions changed to a great extent by 1954.

> In 1956, one poll found that only 14 percent of Southern whites thought that black and white students should attend the same school, and that poll included whites in the Border States and Washington, D.C. With that public opinion in the background, southern states and local governments exercised a variety of legal tactics to forestall any meaningful school integration. The Civil Rights Movement was making inroads through the courts, but even five years after the infamous 1957 standoff in Little Rock, Arkansas, only 1 percent of southern black students attended school with whites. (Francis, n.d., para. 6)

SEGREGATION GROWING

"The growth of segregation has been most dramatic for Latino students, particularly in the West, where there was substantial integration in the 1960s, and segregation has soared. A clear pattern is developing of black and Latino students sharing the same schools; it deserves serious attention from educators and policymakers.

Segregation is typically segregation by both race and poverty. Black and Latino students tend to be in schools with a substantial majority of poor children, but white and Asian students are typically in middle-class schools.

Segregation is by far the most serious in the central cities of the largest metropolitan areas, but it is also severe in central cities of all sizes and suburbs of the largest metro areas, which are now half nonwhite. Latinos are significantly more segregated than blacks in suburban America." (Orfield et al., 2014, para. 4–6)

LESSON 5
WHAT IS LEADERSHIP IN A DEMOCRATIC SOCIETY?

OVERVIEW

LESSON AT A GLANCE

- ➤ Students analyze historical records of the Montgomery Bus Boycott.
- ➤ Students use a concept development strategy to examine the concepts of democratic citizenship and boycott.

TIMELINE EVENTS

- ➤ 1955: Montgomery Bus Boycott

ESSENTIAL QUESTIONS

- ➤ What was the impact of the Montgomery Bus Boycott on desegregation?
- ➤ What is the meaning of democratic citizenship?
- ➤ Who showed leadership during the Montgomery Bus Boycott?
- ➤ In what ways was Rosa Parks a leader for democratic citizenship?

CONCEPTUAL UNDERSTANDINGS

- ➤ Historians examine multiple accounts of an event to draw conclusions.
- ➤ Accounts of historical events are influenced by factors such as availability of factual data, perspectives of data sources, and the credibility of the reporter.
- ➤ Democratic citizens are informed, active participants seeking the common good and a just society.

IMPORTANT TERMS AND IDEAS

- ➤ *segregation*: the separation of people based on race
- ➤ *boycott*: to stop using, buying, or dealing with an individual or group as a protest
- ➤ *misconception*: a common notion that is incorrect
- ➤ *racism*: the mindset that some groups of people are more important or better than others
- ➤ *democratic citizenship*: one who has the rights and privileges granted in a democratic government, especially the right to vote

MATERIALS

➤ Rosa Parks interview: http://www.achievement.org/autodoc/page/par0int-1
➤ Video: *Mighty Times: The Legacy of Rosa Parks*. Available from http://www.tolerance.org/kit/mighty-times-legacy-rosa-parks
➤ Website with interviews and newspaper reports: http://zinnedproject.org/materials/voices-of-the-montgomery-bus-boycott/
➤ Handout 5.1: Interview and Newspaper Accounts Assignments
➤ Handout 5.2: Bus Boycotters Speak Out
➤ Handout 5.3: From the Archives: The Montgomery Bus Boycott
➤ Handout 5.4: Boycott Concept Graphic
➤ Handout 5.5: Democratic Citizenship Concept Graphic

SUGGESTED RESOURCES

➤ Freedman, R. (2010). *Freedom walkers: The story of the Montgomery Bus Boycott. New York, NY:* Holt McDougal.
➤ Giovanni, N. (2005). *Rosa.* New York, NY: Henry Holt.
➤ Theoharis, J. (2014). *The rebellious life of Mrs. Rosa Parks.* Boston, MA: Beacon.
➤ Kohl, H. (2007). *She would not be moved: How we tell the story of Rosa Parks and the Montgomery Bus Boycott.* New York, NY: New Press.
➤ Hoose, P. (2010). *Claudette Colvin: Twice toward justice.* New York City, NY: Farrar, Straus and Giroux.
➤ Parks, R. (1999). *Rosa Parks: My story.* New York, NY: Penguin.
➤ http://memory.loc.gov/ammem/aaohtml/exhibit/aopart9.html#0903

INSTRUCTIONS

1. Prior to this lesson, select students to prepare a dramatic reading of the interview of Rosa Parks available on the Academy of Achievement website (http://www.achievement.org/autodoc/page/par0int-1). Use the section of the interview up to the question, "How old were you?" Provide students with a copy of the interview transcript and give them a short time before class to practice. Prepare a sign with the name "Rosa Parks" and "Interviewer" for the readers to wear. Alternatively, you may show students the video clip of this interview, also available at the Academy of Achievement website or the video *Mighty Times: The Legacy of Rosa Parks*, available at http://www.tolerance.org/kit/mighty-times-legacy-rosa-parks.

THE HOOK

2. Tell students they will have an opportunity to listen to an interview of a very important person in the Civil Rights Movement. Tell them the actual interview was conducted by the Academy of Achievement in 1995. Direct the assigned students to complete the dramatization. After the reading, ask: *Were you familiar with the story of the bus boycott and*

Rosa Parks before this presentation? Why did Rosa Parks decide to engage in this boycott? What do you think about the bus driver? The police officer?

DEVELOPING CONCEPTUAL UNDERSTANDING

3. Tell students that Rosa Parks was not alone in boycotting the buses in Montgomery and, in fact, she was also not the first person to boycott by refusing to comply with the seating requirements for African Americans. Let them know that today they will learn about many more people involved in the boycott. Tell them that they will have access to interviews of people who participated in the Montgomery Bus Boycott as well as news accounts of the boycott. Let them know that they will work together to learn more about what happened and what news reporters had to say.

> *Teacher's Note.* The website http://www.montgomeryboycott.com presents interviews with 25 individuals who participated in or experienced the Montgomery Bus Boycott. If Internet access is available, allow students to complete a search for their assigned interview. If not, prepare copies of selected interviews for small groups to use.

4. Assign students to partners or small groups for the research activities to be completed on the Montgomery Bus Boycotts. Provide each with an assigned person and an assigned news story from the website, http://www.montgomeryboycott.com/. The interviews can be found under "Voices of the Boycott" and the news stories under "Archives." Photos and front-page views of newspapers are also available on the website. Use Handout 5.1 to record and keep track of assignments. Tell students that their task is to learn some interesting things about the person assigned to them and also discover the ways in which the newspapers reported on the boycotts. Provide Handout 5.2: Bus Boycotters Speak Out for student records.

5. Arrange for Internet access or provide copies of interviews to student groups and discuss the importance of historical data in understanding what really happened. Ask:
   a. Will the interviews tell the real story? Why or why not?
   b. As a historian, what data would help you to understand what really happened?
   c. Will your analysis of the group of interviews offer more credible insight? Why or why not?

6. Tell students to read/view their assigned interview and record notes on paper in preparation for completing their report on Handout 5.2. Allow time for research and then ask groups to discuss what they learned in terms of:
   a. actions the person took/saw others take; and
   b. the feelings and thoughts of the person interviewed about the goals of the boycott.

7. Instruct students to complete Handout 5.2 to summarize the information gained from the interview.

8. Next, ask students to read their assigned news report in preparation for a discussion about the Montgomery Bus Boycott. Distribute 5.3: From the Archives: The Montgomery Bus Boycott. Instruct them to look for words that convey the thoughts and opinions of those involved in preparation for a discussion of the events and the people involved. Tell them to take notes to highlight the most important events as well as the perspective of those interviewed. Ask them to look for actions/reactions and list these. Provide time for the reading and note taking in their small groups.

9. Open a class discussion of the boycott. Begin by asking: *What is a boycott?* Project Handout 5.4, the graphic organizer for the concept "boycott," or draw it on chart paper. Ask for examples of boycotts. Next, suggest that students review their notes for characteristics of the Montgomery Bus Boycott and others they know about. Move to the "nonexamples" of boycotts that might be similar or close to a boycott but not exactly. Then ask the small groups to come up with a definition of a boycott. Ask groups to share and seek a class definition.

10. Next, ask students to consider the leadership for the Montgomery Bus Boycott.
    a. Rosa Parks broke a law in order to further the cause. What law did she break? Do you think that this was right?
    b. Was Rosa Parks a democratic citizen?
    c. What other people and organizations were involved in the struggle for equal treatment by the bus company?
    d. How were their roles similar? Different?
    e. How did their different tactics or approaches work together to make change happen?
    f. Who were leaders in this effort? How did they show leadership? How did they become leaders? Why do you think people followed them?
    g. What would have happened if the community decided not to boycott the buses for such a long time?
    h. Were those who boycotted demonstrating democratic citizenship?

11. Project or draw a large version of the graphic for democratic citizenship and provide copies (Handout 5.5) to students. Record "Rosa Parks's actions" in the "examples" quadrant. Elicit other examples from history of democratic citizens or acts that show democratic citizenship and add them to the "examples" quadrant. Ask students if the Montgomery taxi drivers, who lowered their rates to the cost of a bus ride, should be in the examples quadrant.

12. Ask: *What are the characteristics of a democratic citizen?* Record student ideas about the characteristics of democratic citizens on the "essential characteristics" quadrant of the chart.

13. Ask: *Can you think of any nonexamples of democratic citizenship?* Prompting questions if the class has trouble thinking of nonexamples include:
    a. Do you think the bus driver was acting as a democratic citizen? He was trying to uphold the law, after all. Is it always good to uphold laws?
    b. What groups or activities do you recall from history as not exhibiting actions of a democratic citizen?

14. Record student ideas in the "nonexamples" quadrant of the chart. Tell students: Now, discuss with a partner or group the definition portion of this quadrant. Can you list the important elements of democratic citizenship and put them together to form a definition? Invite students to share definitions and create a class definition of democratic citizenship. Post the definition prominently for the remainder of the unit.

15. After a suitable definition is agreed upon, help students to develop a few generalizations about democratic citizenship. Ask students: *What can you say about democratic citizenship that is just about always true? Let's look at the examples and characteristics on our chart to guide our thinking and write some statements that are generalizations.* Ask for ideas and record a statement as an example. Encourage students to discuss in their groups and try to come up with one per group. Record their ideas. Possible generalization examples include:

    a. *Participants*: Citizens can vote, run for office, engage in public service, volunteer, contribute to the economy, pay taxes, serve in the armed forces, serve on a jury, and actively obey laws.

    b. *Informed*: Actively seeking information, reading and understanding the rights and liberties promised in the Declaration of Independence and the U.S. Constitution, understanding the many competing points of view of citizens.

    c. *Public good*: Putting the good of others ahead of self-interest, supporting groups who are marginalized, contributing to others by way of financial help or volunteerism.

    d. *Just society*: Behaving ethically, having a strong sense of right and wrong, taking responsibility for their actions, exercising free will and not preventing others from doing the same, providing a fair distribution of wealth and benefits, an uncorrupted government.

SOAR: SUMMARIZE, OBSERVE, ASSESS, REFLECT

16. After discussing student generalizations, introduce the following ideas as those the class will focus on in the unit. Discuss each idea, using the questions as a guide.

    a. Citizens are active participants in their government (local, state, and national). What situations can you think of that would be examples of this? In what ways do you or people you know participate in the government?

    b. Citizens must be informed in order to effectively participate in the political process. What are some examples? What kinds of things would a citizen need to know? Why would a citizen need this information?

    c. Citizens value the public good. Can you think of examples of people who value the public good? How do citizens demonstrate this?

    d. Democratic citizens strive to create a just society. In what ways do citizens achieve this? Can you think of any examples? What is just?

17. Ask students to record (by letter) which generalizations about democratic citizenship apply to leaders of the Civil Rights Movement. Observe student responses, making note of those having difficulty making connections. Allow volunteers to share their ideas, asking others if they agree or disagree and why. Ask students to reflect on one way in which they might demonstrate strong democratic citizenship in their school and community.

THINK AGAIN (HOMEWORK)

18. Ask students to nominate one person in their own lives or someone famous (living or dead) whose actions represent democratic citizenship and then record their thoughts about why they selected this person, using the generalizations about democratic citizenship to guide their thinking.

19. Or, invite students to consider what they have learned about the Montgomery Bus Boycott and the people involved. Ask them to write a short poem, draw/paint their reaction to the events, or create lyrics to a song as a tribute to a democratic citizen they discovered. This may be their interview person or a group of people such as the riders or those who participated in the boycott.

KEEP ON GOING (LESSON EXTENSIONS)

20. Challenge students to select another example of a democratic citizen who participated in a boycott or other form of protest in the 1950s and write a brief biographical sketch to share with the class in some form (bulletin board, wiki, class webpage, oral report, brief slide presentation, poem, song).

21. Provide students with the following website to read the "Integrated Bus Suggestions" provided by the Montgomery Improvement Association in order to help guide the behaviors of those boarding integrated buses: http://www.archives.alabama.gov/teacher/rights/lesson1/doc7.html. Direct students to read and analyze the suggestions in light of the generalizations about democratic citizenship. Were the bus riders being asked to demonstrate positive democratic citizenship? Ask students to develop and record a list of suggestions for their own school's student bus riders, conveying the principles of democratic citizenship including rights and responsibilities.

HANDOUT 5.1
INTERVIEW AND NEWSPAPER ACCOUNTS ASSIGNMENTS

INTERVIEW ASSIGNMENTS

See website for The Montgomery Bus Boycott: Voices of the Boycott to access the interviews (http://www.montgomeryboycott.com/voices-of-the-boycott/).

Class Reporter	Person	Class Reporter	Person
	Inez Baskin		Lillie Mae Bradford
	Aurelia Coleman		Johnnie Carr
	Samuel Gadson		Fred Gray Sr.
	Thelma Glass		Annie B. Giles
	Urelee Gordon		Rev. Robert Graetz
	Thomas Gray		Amelia Scott Green
	Vera Harris		Charlie Hardy
	Bob Ingram		Sarah Herbert
	Gwen Patton		Dorothy P. Jones
	Idessa Redden		Dorothy Posey & Inell Johnson
	John F. Sawyer, Jr.		E. D. Nixon
	Mary Jo Smiley		
	Lucille Times		
	Rev. Donnie Williams		

Handout 5.1: Interview and Newspaper Accounts Assignments, continued

ARCHIVES FOR THE MONTGOMERY BUS BOYCOTT ASSIGNMENTS

See website for The Montgomery Bus Boycott: Archives to access the articles (http://www.montgomeryboycott.com/archived-articles/).

Class Reporter	Title of Article

HANDOUT 5.2
BUS BOYCOTTERS SPEAK OUT

Name of Person	
Date of Interview	
Issues Discussed	
Questions Asked	
Key Point Shared	
Key Point Shared	
Connections to Civil Rights Movement	

Your reaction: What do you think? What surprised you? How did you feel?

_____

_____

_____

_____

_____

_____

NAME:_____ DATE:_____

HANDOUT 5.3
FROM THE ARCHIVES: THE MONTGOMERY BUS BOYCOTT

Name of Source	
Date	
Headline	
Author	
What is this article about?	
Who was involved?	
Where did it happen?	
Why did it happen?	

Your reaction: What do you think? Was the reporting factual? Do you detect any bias?

_____

_____

_____

_____

_____

_____

HANDOUT 5.4
BOYCOTT CONCEPT GRAPHIC

Examples	Essential Characteristics

BOYCOTT

Nonexamples	Definition

HANDOUT 5.5
DEMOCRATIC CITIZENSHIP CONCEPT GRAPHIC

Examples	Essential Characteristics

DEMOCRATIC CITIZENSHIP

Nonexamples	Definition

Generalizations: _____

_____

_____

_____

LESSON 6
HOW CAN CONFLICT BE RESOLVED WITHOUT VIOLENCE?

OVERVIEW

LESSON AT A GLANCE (2-DAY LESSON)

➤ Students analyze Dr. Martin Luther King Jr.'s "Letter From Birmingham Jail."
➤ On day 1, students read and analyze Dr. Martin Luther King Jr.'s letter.
➤ On day 2, students engage in a Socratic Seminar, considering Dr. King's words and actions in relation to the expectations for democratic citizens and his impact on the quest for equal rights.

TIMELINE EVENTS

➤ April 12, 1963: Statement by Alabama clergymen
➤ April 12, 1963: Arrest of Dr. Martin Luther King Jr. in Birmingham, AL

ESSENTIAL QUESTIONS

➤ How did Dr. King view the Civil Rights Movement?
➤ How did others view the movement?
➤ What was the purpose of this letter?
➤ How can nonviolence bring about change?
➤ What is meant by just/unjust law? When, if ever, is it okay to break an unjust law?

CONCEPTUAL UNDERSTANDINGS

➤ Dr. King's approach to change continues to influence people's efforts to effect change.
➤ Power in societies comes from the consent and compliance of people in those societies. In nonviolent conflict, people change their patterns of consent and obedience, and therefore change their behavior, as a way of exercising power.
➤ Engaging in a reasoned discussion of a reading, event, or experience can lead to a deepened understanding of historical events.
➤ The interpretation of history depends upon more than the reporting and sequencing of events.
➤ Historical documents can reveal issues, ideas, and values.

IMPORTANT TERMS AND IDEAS

- ➤ *confined*: kept against one's will
- ➤ *affiliated*: related to
- ➤ *retaliate*: to get revenge
- ➤ *moratorium*: a period of time in which an activity is halted
- ➤ *nonconformist*: one who does not act in compliance with generally accepted actions
- ➤ *intimidate*: to cause to be fearful, to frighten
- ➤ *harried*: having many worries or problems
- ➤ *latent*: not active or visible at the present time
- ➤ *languish*: to have little progress toward a better situation
- ➤ *provocation*: some action that makes another angry or forces a reaction
- ➤ *passive resistance*: demonstrating opposition without the use of violence
- ➤ *civil disobedience*: to refuse to follow a law because it is believed to be unjust or immoral
- ➤ *just/unjust law*: fair, morally right/unfair, immoral

MATERIALS

- ➤ Handout 6.1: "Letter From Birmingham Jail": Key Ideas
- ➤ Handout 6.2: Statement From Alabama Clergymen
- ➤ Handout 6.3: "Letter From Birmingham Jail" Seminar Ticket
- ➤ Handout 6.4: Socratic Seminar Discussion Guidelines
- ➤ Photograph of Martin Luther King Jr. being arrested in 1962 from http://www.americaslibrary.gov/aa/king/aa_king_jail_1_e.html

SUGGESTED RESOURCES

- ➤ Rieder, J. (2013). *Gospel of freedom: Martin Luther King, Jr.'s Letter from Birmingham Jail and the struggle that changed a nation.* New York, NY: Bloomsbury Press.
- ➤ http://www.sohp.org
- ➤ http://www.thekingcenter.org
- ➤ http://www.cnn.com/SPECIALS/2007/king.papers/
- ➤ http://i.a.cnn.net/cnn/SPECIALS/2007/king.papers/images/jail.rather.bail.pdf

INSTRUCTIONS

THE HOOK

1. Ask students to visualize Dr. Martin Luther King Jr. in action. Allow some volunteers to share what they visualize (Protests? March on Washington? Giving speeches?). Project the picture of Dr. Martin Luther King Jr. being arrested. Ask: *Is this how you think of Dr. Martin Luther King Jr.?* Explain to students that this picture was taken before his famous March on Washington where he delivered the "I Have a Dream" speech. He was arrested for trespassing as part of a demonstration. Let students know that today's lesson will

explore Dr. King's thoughts as he sat in jail another time, in Birmingham, AL. Explain the terms passive resistance and civil disobedience. You might need to emphasize how radical this methodology was at the time.

DEVELOPING CONCEPTUAL UNDERSTANDING

2. Read the first two paragraphs of Dr. King's "Letter From Birmingham Jail" (see link on Handout 6.1). Ask: *Why was Dr. King in Birmingham? What was his mission? What was happening in Birmingham in 1963?* Provide some background on Martin Luther King Jr.'s journey to Birmingham to help lead the demonstrations. You may choose to read and/or project Dr. King's notes on "Jail Not Bail" (see Suggested Resources) to help students understand more about Dr. King's ideas of leadership and justice. Remind students that historians seek historical documents to be able to understand historical events. In this case, pictures and Dr. King's actual words are vital in any analysis. It will also be helpful to look at the statement to which Dr. King was responding with his "Letter From Birmingham Jail."

3. Distribute the Statement From Alabama Clergymen (Handout 6.2). Inform students that this is a copy of the actual statement written by Alabama clergymen and directed to Dr. King. Ask students to read it silently or direct them to take turns reading it aloud. Ask students to follow along and circle any vocabulary they do not understand.

4. Use these document analysis questions:
   - Who is the author(s) of the document?
   - What does the letter tell us about the events in Birmingham and the perspective of the authors (evidence)?
   - What do we learn from this evidence?
   - What are the limitations of this evidence? What else do we want to learn/know?

5. Explain that this analysis will help students prepare for the Socratic Seminar that they are going to participate in tomorrow. Follow the reading with a brief class discussion, including an analysis of any words that were confusing.

6. Tell students: *Tomorrow you will participate in a seminar on Dr. Martin Luther King Jr.'s "Letter From Birmingham Jail," his response to the Alabama clergymen. A seminar is a discussion group in which well-informed people talk about an event or an issue in order to understand it more thoroughly, especially the ideas and values presented in the reading. Although people may have different interpretations or opinions, the purpose of a seminar is not to debate, but rather to put together the collective understanding of the group. We can learn from each other as we discuss the issues and our understanding of them. In a seminar, there are no right or wrong answers. To be well-informed, you must prepare ahead of time. That means you will need to do some work and come to class with your "ticket," that is, your preparatory notes on the reading. Usually when we have discussions I lead them, but in a seminar you all are responsible for the discussion. I will only be here to facilitate, to keep things going, but not to ask the questions. Because you will be in charge of the discussion, you will need to prepare very well. You must bring your ticket to join the discussion. Our seminar will be about the events that occurred in Birmingham in 1963. So let's begin the preparations.*

7. Give students Dr. King's "Letter From Birmingham Jail": Key Ideas (Handout 6.1) and the Socratic Seminar ticket for this work (Handout 6.3). Print copies of the "Letter From Birmingham Jail" from the link provided, then read it aloud while students follow along, starting with the third paragraph. Ask students to mark up the text with questions, identify unfamiliar words, or chart initial reactions. You may want to show an example of your own marked-up text as a model.

8. Guide students' thinking by modeling and asking questions such as:
    - What are the injustices Dr. King speaks of?
    - What different forms of response to injustice does Dr. King discuss?
    - What different emotions does Dr. King reveal?
    - What emotions do readers feel?
    - What examples of violence does he share?
    - What does he believe is the "truth"?

9. Review the seminar ticket with the students and instruct them to read the text again before starting their work. Direct students to work in a partnership or small group.

THINK AGAIN: HOMEWORK FOR DAY ONE

10. Ask students to complete their preparation for the Socratic Seminar for homework. Remind them that their preparation will be their ticket for admission to the seminar.

DAY 2: SOCRATIC SEMINAR

11. Ask students to talk with the person next to them as a warm-up for the discussion, sharing one of their responses to the questions on the seminar ticket as well as some of their vocabulary words. Ask students to suggest questions that would be good seminar questions and put together a list on the board. Limit the number of questions and indicate that they may not address all of the questions during the seminar, but the questions will be helpful if they need prompts to maintain the discussion.

Teacher's Note. To prepare the students and the classroom for the seminar, arrange students in a circle facing one another. This is done so that all students are on an equal plane for the discussion.

If the group is larger than 20, arrange two circles, an inner circle and an outer one. The inner circle engages in the discussion and the outer circle is given a directed listening assignment, such as recording important points made by the speakers and reflecting on the effectiveness of the discussion in general.

If two circles are used, direct students from the outer circle to exchange seats with those in the inner circle midway through the discussion. Students who come unprepared should remain in the outer circle and/or work on their assignment.

You might also consider pairing each inner circle student with an outer circle student, asking the outer circle to take a few notes on their partner's participation and then giving factual feedback at the end of the round. The positions and feedback would be reversed in the second round of discussion.

12. Review the guidelines for an effective Socratic Seminar (Handout 6.5). Emphasize the purpose for the seminar—to develop good discussion skills and gain a better understanding of the issues, ideas, and values of the text. Begin the seminar by posing an opening question. Suggested questions for initiating the discussion include:
     *   What is the purpose of this letter?
     *   Who is the audience or audiences of this letter?
     *   How does King differentiate a just from unjust law?
     *   According to Dr. King, is it ever appropriate to break an unjust law?

     You may want to read parts of the letter and pause, asking students for what they understand the message to be in this part of the letter.

     Teacher's Note. When discussion starts to taper off or you feel you have gone far enough on a particular topic, pose another question.
     *   Let students lead the direction of the discussion.
     *   Invite others to participate if several students are dominating or to help summarize the students' main points.
     *   Allow the discussion to veer away from the question list if it is productive.
     *   Seek quality of responses, not quantity. It is not necessary to get through the list of questions.
     *   Allow time for a summary question.
     *   A good seminar leaves students with more to say on the topic and more ideas to include in the seminar response. Don't expect a neat closure. Hopefully students will continue discussing these ideas on their own.

SOAR: SUMMARIZE, OBSERVE, ASSESS, REFLECT

13. Ask students to turn to the person next to them and share any ideas or thoughts they did not get a chance to share. Ask students the following: *How do you think the seminar went today? What did we do well? How can we do better next time?*

THINK AGAIN: HOMEWORK FOR DAY TWO

14. Allow students to choose one of the following seminar response activities to complete.
     *   Is there such a thing as an unjust law in a democracy? Under what conditions might it be necessary for a democratic citizen to break an unjust law?
     *   You are a citizen of Birmingham in 1963. Write your own letter to the paper's editor responding to both King and the White clergy who posted the original letter.

KEEP ON GOING: LESSON EXTENSIONS

15. Challenge students to identify other people (Suggestions: Nelson Mandela, Gandhi, Cesar Chavez, Dalai Lama) who used nonviolence as a powerful approach to leadership for change. Ask them to select one person or movement and develop a profile including a photo, key points related to the cause and the approach used, and quotes related to the nonviolent approach.

HANDOUT 6.1
"LETTER FROM BIRMINGHAM JAIL": KEY IDEAS

Dr. Martin Luther King Jr. wrote this letter from jail, having been arrested for his nonviolent protesting against racial segregation in Birmingham, AL. He was writing in response to the public statement made by the eight clergymen from Alabama.

Locate excerpts from Dr. King's letter at http://teachingamericanhistory.org/library/document/letter-from-birmingham-city-jail-excerpts/ or other websites that include the entire document.

Read Dr. King's letter to locate passages that support each of the following statements:

➤ People have a responsibility to help each other combat injustice no matter where it occurs.
➤ Nonviolence requires planning and action in a specific way.
➤ Direct action is required when circumstances merit it and will result in progress.
➤ Freedom requires action.
➤ Waiting may not be the best action in all cases.
➤ Extremism is sometimes necessary.

HANDOUT 6.2
STATEMENT FROM ALABAMA CLERGYMEN

The following is a public statement directed to Martin Luther King Jr. by eight Alabama clergymen.

A Group of Clergymen
April 12, 1963

We clergymen are among those who, in January, issued "an Appeal for Law and Order and Common Sense," in dealing with racial problems in Alabama. We expressed understanding that honest convictions in racial matters could properly be pursued in the courts, but urged that decisions of those courts should in the meantime be peacefully obeyed.

Since that time there has been some evidence of increased forbearance and a willingness to face facts. Responsible citizens have undertaken to work on various problems which cause racial friction and unrest. In Birmingham, recent public events have given indication that we all have opportunity for a new constructive and realistic approach to racial problems.

However, we are now confronted by a series of demonstrations by some of our Negro citizens, directed and led in part by outsiders. We recognize the natural impatience of people who feel that their hopes are slow in being realized. But we are convinced that these demonstrations are unwise and untimely.

We agree rather with certain local Negro leadership which has called for honest and open negotiation of racial issues in our area. And we believe this kind of facing of issues can best be accomplished by citizens of our own metropolitan area, white and Negro, meeting with their knowledge and experiences of the local situation. All of us need to face that responsibility and find proper channels for its accomplishment.

Just as we formerly pointed out that "hatred and violence have no sanction in our religious and political traditions," we also point out that such actions as incite to hatred and violence, however technically peaceful those actions may be, have not contributed to the resolution of our local problems. We do not believe that these days of new hope are days when extreme measures are justified in Birmingham.

We commend the community as a whole, and the local news media and law enforcement officials in particular, on the calm manner in which these demonstrations have been handled. We urge the public to continue to show restraint should the demonstrations continue, and the law enforcement officials to remain calm and continue to protect our city from violence.

We further strongly urge our own Negro community to withdraw support from these demonstrations, and to unite locally in working peacefully for a better Birmingham. When rights are consistently denied, a cause should be pressed in the courts and in negotiations among local leaders, and not in the streets. We appeal to both our white and Negro citizenry to observe the principles of law and order and common sense.

Signed by:
C.C.J. CARPENTER, D.D., LL.D., Bishop of Alabama.
JOSEPH A. DURICK, D.D., Auxiliary Bishop, Diocese of Mobile-Birmingham
Rabbi MILTON L. GRAFMAN, Temple Emanu-El, Birmingham, Alabama
Bishop PAUL HARDIN, Bishop of the Alabama-West Florida Conference of the Methodist Church
Bishop NOLAN B. HARMON, Bishop of the North Alabama Conference of the Methodist Church
GEORGE M. MURRAY, D.D., LL.D., Bishop Coadjutor, Episcopal Diocese of Alabama
EDWARD V. RAMAGE, Moderator, Synod of the Alabama Presbyterian Church in the United States
EARL STALLINGS, Pastors, First Baptist Church, Birmingham, Alabama

HANDOUT 6.3
"LETTER FROM BIRMINGHAM JAIL" SEMINAR TICKET

Directions: Read the letter twice before writing anything on this sheet. The second time you read, highlight or underline words or phrases that you think are important, puzzling, or intriguing to you. Make notes in the margins about your thoughts and feelings as you read the passage and any questions you have about what the text says.

1. Identify any words that you do not understand or think are important to the text. Give the meaning and an original sentence for each word.

Word	Meaning and Sentence

2. What is the purpose of this letter?

_____

_____

3. Who is Dr. King's audience(s) for this letter?

_____

_____

4. How does Dr. King describe a just from unjust law?

_____

_____

5. Write two additional open-ended questions that require discussion. Do not ask questions with right or wrong answers or ones that can be answered by simply looking at the text.

a. _____

_____

b. _____

_____

HANDOUT 6.4
SOCRATIC SEMINAR
DISCUSSION GUIDELINES

Socratic Seminar Discussion Guidelines	
The seminar requires careful preparation.	"Buy" your ticket.
The seminar is a thoughtful conversation.	Speak one at a time.
The seminar requires careful listening.	Listen for important points.
The seminar is a student discussion.	Speak to each other, not to the teacher.
The seminar is based on evidence.	Back up your ideas with text citations.
The seminar is a thinking activity.	No answer is "right" or "wrong."

GUIDING PHRASES

You may find the following phrases useful in helping you participate in a thoughtful discussion.

If you agree, say:
➤ I have the same opinion because . . .
➤ I found the same thing in the reading . . .
➤ What (Name) says agrees with what I believe because . . .

If you disagree, say:
➤ (Name)'s opinion is different from mine because . . .
➤ I found something different. It says . . .
➤ I disagree because . . .
➤ My interpretation differs in this way . . .
➤ I don't think it meant that because . . .

If you don't understand, say:
➤ I am not sure I understand. Can you explain that in a different way?
➤ I think I understand, but is this what you are saying? (Follow with rephrasing the explanation)
➤ When you say _____ what exactly do you mean?
➤ Can you clarify that?

When you have a general question or comment, say:
➤ I have another point I would like to make.
➤ I have a question that I think relates to what we are saying.
➤ I wonder about _____.
➤ Did anyone else think _____?

LESSON 7
CAN CHILDREN BE CHANGE AGENTS FOR EQUAL RIGHTS?

OVERVIEW

LESSON AT A GLANCE

➤ Students view the video *Mighty Times: The Children's March* and record personal reflections on what happened. They analyze their feelings about the events and share their impressions in a class discussion.

TIMELINE EVENTS

➤ 1963: Children's March

ESSENTIAL QUESTIONS

➤ What is the price of acting on your beliefs?
➤ How do people's different views of democratic citizenship impact their actions?
➤ In what ways did participants in the Civil Rights Movement display leadership?

CONCEPTUAL UNDERSTANDINGS

➤ Change occurs in a society when people unite to accomplish common goals.
➤ Public protests have the power to influence public sentiments, both positively and negatively.
➤ Boycotts can effect change through social and economic impact.

IMPORTANT TERMS AND IDEAS

➤ *civil disobedience*: refusing to follow a law because it is regarded as unfair or immoral
➤ *documentary*: film presentation showing a factual account of an event, life, or period of time

MATERIALS

➤ *Mighty Times: The Children's March* DVD (40 minutes) available free of charge from Teaching Tolerance at http://www.tolerance.org/kit/mighty-times-childrens-march
➤ DVD player and projector

➤ Handout 7.1: Mighty Times: The Children's March Note-Taking Chart

SUGGESTED RESOURCES

➤ Levinson, C. (2012). *We've got a job: The 1963 Birmingham Children's March.* Atlanta, GA: Peachtree.

➤ Theunissen, S. (2102). *Through Angel's eyes.* Houston, TX: Strategic Book.

➤ Webb-Christburg, S., Nelson, R., & Sikora, F. (1997). *Selma, Lord, Selma: Girlhood memories of the civil rights days.* Tuscaloosa: University of Alabama Press.

➤ Fradin, J. B., & Fradin, D. B. (2004). *The power of one: Daisy Bates and the Little Rock Nine.* New York, NY: Clarion Books.

➤ Partridge, E. (2009). *Marching for freedom: Walk together, children, and don't you grow weary.* New York, NY: Viking.

➤ Tillage, L. (2000). *Leon's story.* New York, NY: Farar, Strauss, & Giroux.

➤ Thomas, J. C., & James, C. (2003). *Linda Brown, you are not alone: The Brown v. Board of Education decision.* New York, NY: Jump At The Sun.

➤ http://www.thedailybeast.com/articles/2013/05/02/how-the-children-of-birmingham-changed-the-civil-rights-movement.html

➤ http://mlk-kpp01.stanford.edu/index.php/encyclopedia/encyclopedia/enc_childrens_crusade/

INSTRUCTIONS

THE HOOK

1. Ask students to imagine the following scenario: *You are Dr. Martin Luther King Jr. and it is 1963. You have spent the last 8 days in a jail cell in Birmingham, AL, because you were marching on behalf of the African American citizens of Birmingham. The Birmingham residents who marched with you are all in jail, too. To help pass the time while you are in jail, you write a response to the statement by local White ministers who condemned your actions. This response was to become known as the "Letter From Birmingham Jail." Finally the day has come for you to be released from jail. You will finally be able to see your family and friends again. You're excited to see how the people of Birmingham want to help move this campaign forward and fight for their rights. Yet when you sit down to meet with community leaders and leaders in the SCLC (Southern Christian Leadership Conference), it becomes clear that most of the people of Birmingham are too afraid to march. They fear that they will lose their jobs either because of retaliation by angry White employers or be unable to work if they get arrested. These people know they must continue to work to support their families.*

2. *What could Dr. King and the SCLC do to solve this problem and keep moving the Birmingham campaign forward?* Discuss student ideas. Tell them that the SCLC with Dr. King's support found a way to move the campaign forward, with the help of its youngest citizens.

DEVELOPING CONCEPTUAL UNDERSTANDING

3. Ask students if they have ever seen a documentary on TV or at the movies. Ask for a definition of "documentary." If students are unable to explain the term, offer them some examples of documentary titles:
    - *Food, Inc.*: A story of agribusiness and its devastating economic and environmental effects.
    - *Tent City*: A perspective on the plight of the homeless in a New Jersey community.
    - *America's Great Indian Leaders*: A story of the end of the American Indian's traditional way of life.
    - *Sicko*: An exploration of the horrors of the American health care industry.

    Guide students to an understanding of a documentary as a video or radio program providing a factual report.

4. Tell students that it is difficult for us to imagine what some African American families went through in the time of the Civil Rights Movement, but that a good documentary can give them a window into that world. When the Birmingham efforts were falling apart because of adults being jailed, the leaders turned to the children to help. Let students know that you have found a documentary called *Mighty Times: The Children's March*, which tells the story of some young people who stood up for their rights during this time. Ask them to consider how much courage it might take for children to become part of protests such as sit-ins, marches, boycotts of local merchants, and mass meetings. How much impact do you think the children might have had on changing the practices that denied full rights to African Americans?

5. Distribute copies of Handout 7.1: *Mighty Times: The Children's March* Note-Taking Chart and ask students to take some notes as they watch the first half of this documentary. Their notes will help them remember their thoughts and feelings as they watch the film. Ask them to write down just enough to jog their memories as they watch the first half of the video. This film may cause strong emotional reactions in some children. This activity is meant to help students reflect upon and process these emotions.

6. Pause the film after the first day of the march; this is about the 22-minute mark in the film and just after the radio disc jockey says, "If today was D-Day, then tomorrow is doubly D-Day." Discuss the righthand side of the notes sheet, Leadership/Democratic Citizenship. Ask:
    - Which people did you identify as leaders who showed democratic citizenship?
    - Why did you choose these people?
    - Which generalizations about democratic citizenship apply to these people?

7. Resume watching the film. Afterward, give students a few minutes to review the notes they have taken. Students should reflect on the Feelings/Emotions side of the chart and write a sentence or two that summarizes the feelings displayed by the people in the film and their own feelings as they viewed it.

8. When students have finished recording their reflections, give them an opportunity to share their thoughts. Acknowledge their feelings and listen to their reflections on the

impact the film had on the people who actually participated in the march or experienced it.

9. Ask the students if they would have gone to the march if they had been living in Birmingham at the time. Continue the discussion, using some of the questions suggested in the teacher's guide to *Mighty Times: The Children's March*. Be sure to incorporate questions that focus their thoughts on the concept of democratic citizenship in relation to the actions of the participants.

SOAR: SUMMARIZE, OBSERVE, ASSESS, REFLECT

10. Conclude the discussion by asking, "According to the film, what were the short- and long-term impacts of the Children's March? What does this tell us about democratic citizenship?" Then ask students to record their thoughts on the question: "Was the Birmingham Campaign a success? Why or why not?" Ask students to turn in their reflections. As you read their comments, look for connections to the concepts of democratic citizenship, civil disobedience, just and unjust laws, and leadership for positive change. Provide feedback to the class on the ideas they have surfaced about this march and its connections to the greater Civil Rights Movement.

THINK AGAIN: HOMEWORK

11. Ask students to share their experience in viewing the film with someone at home. Ask if anyone at home remembers this period of time. If no one knows about this march or other Civil Rights Movement happenings, tell students to share what they learned and get their family's impressions of the event.

KEEP ON GOING: LESSON EXTENSIONS

12. Young students often find ways to support a cause that will positively impact society. Challenge students to find and report on a story of one student or a group of students who saw something that they considered important enough for them to go out of their way to make a difference. Let them know they may research multiple sources such as interviews, newspapers, videos, books, etc. to find a worthy story that is current or from the past.

HANDOUT 7.1
MIGHTY TIMES: THE CHILDREN'S MARCH NOTE-TAKING CHART

Directions: Fill in this chart while you watch the film, *Mighty Times: The Children's March*.

On the Feelings/Emotions side of the chart, describe how the characters in the film are feeling and how you are feeling about the events going on in the film. On the Leadership/Democratic Citizenship side of the chart, write down *who* is showing the characteristics of a democratic citizen leader and *what* they are doing to show their leadership. These are just "reminder notes" for you. You will be thinking, talking, and writing more about these things after the film.

Feelings/Emotions	Leadership/Democratic Citizenship

LESSON 8
HOW DID SOCIAL AND LEGAL INTERVENTIONS INTERSECT IN THE FIGHT FOR CIVIL RIGHTS?

OVERVIEW

LESSON AT A GLANCE

➤ Students analyze artwork depicting civil rights issues
➤ Students examine three important interventions that were used to ensure the civil rights of all citizens:
  • Legislation including the Civil Rights Act of 1964 and the Voting Rights Act of 1965
  • Federal action to enforce voting rights
  • Nonviolent protests and their impact

TIMELINE EVENTS

➤ 1963: Birmingham campaign and Children's March
➤ 1964: Freedom Summer in Mississippi
➤ 1964: Civil Rights Act
➤ 1965: Voting Rights Act
➤ 1965: Selma to Montgomery March

ESSENTIAL QUESTIONS

➤ How do artists contribute to our understanding of historical events?
➤ How do people in a democratic society influence changes in laws?
➤ How do people in a democratic society influence the enforcement of laws?
➤ What is the importance of the right to vote in a democratic society?
➤ What is the role of the federal government in ensuring civil rights?
➤ How does culture influence change?

CONCEPTUAL UNDERSTANDINGS

➤ Emotional reactions to violent and nonviolent events are sometimes communicated through writing, art, and music.
➤ Social issues often inspire overt reactions among all ages and groups of people.
➤ Legislation remains ineffective without the consent of the governed.

IMPORTANT TERMS AND IDEAS

- ➤ *rebellion*: organized resistance to the government
- ➤ *confrontation*: a hostile meeting or situation
- ➤ *legislation*: the body of laws governing citizens

MATERIALS

- ➤ Artwork:
  - *Dixie Café* by Jacob Lawrence, 1948: http://africanamericanart.si.edu/items/show/14
  - *Untitled* by Charles White, 1950: http://africanamericanart.si.edu/items/show/15
  - *Walking* by Charles Henry Alston, 1958: http://africanamericanart.si.edu/items/show/18
  - *Evening Rendezvous* by Norman Lewis, 1962: http://africanamericanart.si.edu/items/show/23
  - *The Problem We All Live With* by Norman Rockwell, 1963: http://collections.nrm.org/search.do?id=320673&db=object&view=detail
  - *Murder in Mississippi* by Norman Rockwell, 1965: http://collections.nrm.org/search.do?id=325055&db=object&view=detail

- ➤ Handout 8.1: Summary of Civil Rights Act of 1964
- ➤ Handout 8.2 Summary of the Voting Rights Act (1965)

SUGGESTED RESOURCES

- ➤ Film: *Selma, Lord, Selma* (1999). An 11-year-old girl, inspired by Dr. Martin Luther King Jr. joins in the march from Selma to Montgomery (94 minutes).
- ➤ http://www.pophistorydig.com/topics/%E2%80%9Crockwell-race%E2%80%9D1963-1968/
- ➤ http://www.archives.gov/education/lessons/civil-rights-act/
- ➤ http://www.history.com/topics/black-history/civil-rights-act
- ➤ http://www.congresslink.org/print_basics_histmats_civilrights64text.htm

INSTRUCTIONS

THE HOOK

1. Ask students if they are familiar with the work of Norman Rockwell. Project one or two popular images of his work. Then project his painting entitled "The Problem We All Live With." Ask:
   - Who is the artist?
   - What is pictured in this artwork?
   - What was happening?
   - What details do you notice?

- What story was Rockwell trying to tell?
- What else was happening in the South at this time?

Tell students that the girl in the painting is Ruby Bridges. Encourage them to share what they know about her. Next show a few of the other art images from the African American Art website (see Materials section) and ask students to look for the author's message. Note the year each work was completed and guide students to consider the events occurring in the South around that time.

DEVELOPING CONCEPTUAL UNDERSTANDING

2. Tell students that in today's lesson they will continue to learn about some of the extraordinary efforts some people made in order for all Americans to be able to exercise their rights, particularly the right to vote. Tell students: *The summer of 1964 was known as Freedom Summer in Mississippi or the Mississippi Summer Project. During that summer, leaders attempted to register as many African American voters as possible in the state, since Mississippi had the lowest percentage of African American registered voters in the country. In the South, African Americans were kept from voting by such tactics as poll taxes, difficult literacy tests, inconvenient application processing, harassment, and actions such as arson, beatings, and lynching. Earlier work in Mississippi had resulted in the integration of public accommodations and the organization of local leadership. The Summer Project worked to recruit volunteers from out of state, mostly White, to participate with thousands of Black Mississippians. The volunteers were frequently harassed by White residents of Mississippi who resented the attempts by outsiders to change things in their state. Even state and local government officials, including police, participated in intimidation through arrests, beatings, evictions, and even murder. These were very clear efforts to prevent Blacks from registering to vote, a violation of their civil rights. During this Mississippi summer, several civil rights workers were killed, four people were injured critically, 80 workers were beaten, 1,062 people were arrested, 37 churches were bombed or burned, and 30 homes or businesses were bombed or burned.*

3. Next, show students Rockwell's painting entitled, "Murder in Mississippi." Tell them that this work of art was in response to the events that happened in Mississippi in 1964. Ask:
    - Can you guess who painted this work?
    - Its title is "Murder in Mississippi." What do you notice?
    - What events were likely being depicted?
    - What details support the story?

Tell students that this painting, also done by Rockwell, was based on his understanding of the event. He did his homework prior to painting this picture, writing biographies of the three civil rights workers murdered. He also read articles about the murders and the trials. Ask students to compare Rockwell's two paintings in terms of their details and the stories they tell.

4. Tell students: *News coverage of campaigns like the Children's March, the March on Washington, and the Freedom Summer efforts, in addition to the integration efforts by stu-*

93

dents throughout the United States, kept the civil rights struggle at the forefront of American consciousness. The murders of James Chaney, Andrew Goodman, and Michael Schwerner added to public outcry against the violent reactions to peaceful efforts toward civil rights. Shortly after the Birmingham Campaign, President Kennedy, in a televised address to the nation, outlined his proposed civil rights legislation. This proposed bill would become the Civil Rights Act of 1964, signed into law after his death. It took a great deal of social pressure from groups like SCLC, the NAACP, and CORE (including the famous March on Washington) as well as efforts by President Lyndon B. Johnson and members of Congress for this bill to become law. Because of continued disenfranchisement and violence, President Johnson and Congress became determined to pass legislation requiring states to enforce the 15th Amendment. This legislation was passed in 1965 as the Voting Rights Act.

5. Assign students to small groups and provide groups with one of the Civil Rights Act of 1964 summary statements from Handout 8.1. Ask one person from each group to read the statement to his or her group and allow others to discuss what the statement means and the implications for Americans. Allow time for small groups to complete their discussion and then read each statement in turn, asking groups assigned the statement to explain its meaning and implications. Ask students: *Do you think the Civil Rights Act finally resulted in equal rights and protection for those citizens whose rights had been violated in the past?*

6. Tell students: *In the days following the passage of the Civil Rights Act, the Student Nonviolent Coordinating Committee (SNCC) encountered hostile government officials and widespread fear from African American citizens in Selma, AL, when trying to register to vote (similar to that described in the introduction of this lesson). The Southern Christian Leadership Conference (SCLC) then began a statewide campaign to encourage African Americans to register to vote. This included the march from Selma to Montgomery, AL, to demand just voter registration practices.* Show the video clip of newsreels about the Selma to Montgomery March found on the Eyes on the Prize website: http://www.pbs.org/wgbh/amex/eyesontheprize/story/10_march.html. Discuss the video clip:
   * What were the marchers seeking?
   * Why weren't they getting it?
   * Do you think it was right for the marcher to walk into the state troopers in the first march?
   * Do you think it was right for King to secretly arrange to have the second march cancelled?
   * How did this put pressure on the federal government?
   * How was this effort similar to other campaigns by King and the SCLC? How was it different?

7. Tell students: *This dramatic confrontation, as you can see from the video clip, was featured on television news programs all over the country. This kind of public brutality once again shocked the nation; just as footage of children being attacked by fire hoses and dogs had shocked the public during the Birmingham Campaign. In light of the resulting public outcry, Congress got to work drafting the Voting Rights Act of 1965, which strengthened the voting provisions of the Civil Rights Act of 1964. The Voting Rights Act outlawed the use of literacy*

tests and authorized federal examiners to oversee the registration process in districts with a low percentage of registered voters in any one ethnic group.

SOAR: SUMMARIZE, OBSERVE, ASSESS, REFLECT

8. Post this sentence: *The ability of African Americans to fully and freely participate in government and enjoy the rights of all democratic citizens was an evolutionary process rather than a revolution.* Ask: *Do you think this is a true statement? Talk it over with your small group.* Allow a few minutes for small groups to think through the statement. Help those who need an interpretation of the terms evolutionary and revolution, asking how they differ. Encourage students to think of examples from what they have learned to support their opinion.

THINK AGAIN: HOMEWORK

9. Provide students with Handout 8.2: Summary of the Voting Rights Act (1965). Ask them to read through the summary and pay close attention to the information on Section 5. Write a paragraph explaining why you believe it will be important for you to become a voter when you are of age.

KEEP ON GOING: LESSON EXTENSIONS

10. Students who would benefit from additional challenges and those with interest in the voting rights of today's citizens should be guided to learn more about voting in the United States. Who directs voting? Who monitors it? How does an individual document his or her right to vote? Can voting rights be taken away? Who handles elections? How are votes secured and counted? Students should prepare a brief booklet on voting and voting rights to share with the class.

HANDOUT 8.1
SUMMARY OF CIVIL RIGHTS ACT OF 1964

Directions. Cut the following statements apart and give one to each group.

- -

Title II

Outlawed discrimination in hotels, motels, restaurants, theaters, and all other public accommodations engaged in interstate commerce; exempted private clubs without defining "private," thereby allowing a loophole.

- -

Title III

Encouraged the desegregation of public schools and authorized the U.S. Attorney General to file suits to force desegregation, but did not authorize busing as a means to cover come segregation based on residence.

- -

Title IV

Authorized but did not require withdrawal of federal funds from programs which practiced discrimination.

- -

Title V

Outlawed discrimination in employment in any business exceeding twenty-five people and creates an Equal Opportunities Commission to review complaints, although it lacked meaningful enforcement powers.

- -

Note. Reprinted courtesy of the Dirksen Congressional Center.

HANDOUT 8.2
SUMMARY OF THE VOTING RIGHTS ACT (1965)

The Voting Rights Act of 1965, passed in the wake of voting demonstrations in Selma, Alabama, provided the capstone to many years' efforts to strengthen voting rights for African-Americans. It gave the Attorney General the power to appoint federal examiners to supervise voter registration in states or voting districts where a literacy or other qualifying test was in use and where fewer than 50 percent of voting age residents were registered or had voted in 1964. Eight states were affected in a major way: Alabama, Alaska, Georgia, Louisiana, Mississippi, North Carolina, South Carolina, and Virginia.

Although it may not seem such a radical concept now, the Voting Rights Act departed from the pattern of civil rights bills by providing for direct federal action to enable African-Americans to register and vote. Previous laws required individuals to file suits in courts, a process that often took years to conclude.

Note. Reprinted courtesy of the Dirksen Congressional Center.

LESSON 9
MODERATION OR MILITANCY: IS A CHOICE NECESSARY?

OVERVIEW

LESSON AT A GLANCE

➤ Students compare and contrast the messages and methods of Dr. Martin Luther King Jr. and Malcolm X.

➤ Students explore the actions of both men in relation to an Escalation Model for examining political actions in protest.

TIMELINE EVENTS

➤ 1962: SCLC began protest actions in Birmingham, AL

➤ 1963: Dr. Martin Luther King Jr. arrested in Birmingham, AL

➤ 1964: Malcolm X and Martin Luther King Jr. meet only one time

➤ 1964: Malcolm X forms Organization for Afro-American Unity

ESSENTIAL QUESTIONS

➤ What factors do leaders consider in selecting forms of protest?

➤ How do people in a democratic society influence changes in laws?

CONCEPTUAL UNDERSTANDINGS

➤ Civil disobedience is a direct, yet passive form of resistance.

➤ Groups who formed to bring about desegregation chose different means to the same ends.

➤ Leadership without followers is doomed to failure.

IMPORTANT TERMS AND IDEAS

➤ *militant*: one who uses aggressive actions in support of a political or social cause

➤ *Black Panthers*: revolutionary Black nationalist organization

➤ *resistance*: act of opposing

➤ *activist*: strong advocate for a particular political or social cause

MATERIALS

➤ Audio recording of excerpt from "The Black Revolution Requires Bloodshed": Malcolm X Speech: https://www.marxists.org/reference/archive/malcolm-x/

➤ Or Youtube recording of Malcolm X Speech: https://www.youtube.com/watch?v=ZDW-MHbzORY (Audio and video at the 8:15 to 11:00 mark)

➤ Balloon

➤ Handout 9.1: Escalation Model (Enlarge for posting at the front of the classroom)

➤ Handout 9.2: Malcolm X Speech: "A Message to the Grassroots"

➤ Handout 9.3: Historical Evidence Form

➤ Handout 9.4: Research on Malcolm X

➤ Handout 9.5: Hear My Voice

➤ Handout 9.6: Hear My Voice Answer Key

➤ Handout 9.7: Planning for Equal Rights: Goals, Messages, Actions

➤ Handout 9.8: People of the Civil Rights Movement

SUGGESTED RESOURCES

➤ Breitman, G. (Ed.). (1994). *Malcolm X speaks: Selected speeches and statements.* New York, NY: Grove Press.

➤ Myers, W. D. (1994). *Malcolm X: By any means necessary.* New York, NY: Scholastic.

➤ http://www.pbs.org/wgbh/amex/eyesontheprize/resources/res_video.html

➤ http://www.pbs.org/wgbh/amex/eyesontheprize/about/pt.html

INTRODUCTION

THE HOOK

1. Display Handout 9.1: Escalation Model (enlarged) at the front of the classroom. Make no initial reference to it. Ask students to think about this question, "In what way is blowing up a balloon like the Civil Rights Movement?"

2. Take a balloon and blow it up until it bursts or is ready to burst. Again ask students the question and encourage their comparisons. Ask them if they can compare the Civil Rights Movement to something else, like: How is the Civil Rights Movement like a car's accelerator? How is it like a can of soda? After a few minutes of sharing analogies, refer to the Escalation Model poster.

3. Ask students if they have seen this model before. (Note that this model was developed in a previous unit, *Engaging with History in the Classroom: The Civil War*, in a lesson on the reactions of people to the antislavery movement.) Encourage students to explain what this model represents and how it can be applied to some situations like the Civil War, a disagreement among classmates, etc.

DEVELOPING CONCEPTUAL UNDERSTANDING

4. Ask: *In what situations do you think people have a right to use violence in settling disputes?* Engage students in a class discussion in which students cite examples and reasons for violence/nonviolence. Record their ideas on the board or on chart paper. After a brief discussion, tell students that in today's lesson they will look at evidence from historical documents to answer a similar question.

5. Tell students that their familiarity with the work of Dr. Martin Luther King Jr. will help them to understand another civil rights leader, Malcolm X, since they had similar concerns about democratic citizenship and equality. Explain to students that in this lesson they will be comparing the messages, goals, and methods of these two individuals who significantly impacted the Civil Rights Movement.

6. Display a blank T-chart. Ask students to help you make a list of Dr. Martin Luther King Jr.'s goals (end of racial segregation; ability to exercise 13th, 14th, and 15th Amendment rights; equal treatment). Record their ideas in the lefthand column of the chart. Put a title on this list, "Dr. King's Goals." Above that list, add, "Malcolm X's Goals." Tell students that both of these men had the same hopes and dreams. Next, add a second column to the chart entitled, "Methods." Ask students to help you list Dr. King's methods for reaching these goals (sit-ins, boycotts, marches, rallies, speeches, fill the jails, nonviolence). Label this column, "Dr. King's Methods." Ask students if they think that you should add Malcolm X's name to this column. Ask what evidence they have for their opinion about Malcolm X.

7. Tell students that their real work as historians today will be to analyze historical documents to find out about Malcolm X's messages, goals, and actions. Provide students with an introduction to activism and Malcolm X, a human rights activist, spokesperson, and leader during Civil Rights Movement. Project the text from his "Message to the Grassroots" speech (Handout 9.2). Play the Youtube or audio clip or read the speech aloud and ask students to follow along with the printed copy of the speech. Explain to students that many individuals and groups, including the Black Panthers, became part of the movement that grew from Malcolm X's call for an approach to gaining equality through more violent action than Dr. Martin Luther King Jr. Tell students that the information they receive from studying the documents will help the class to consider the similarities and differences between Dr. Martin Luther King Jr.'s and Malcolm X's approaches.

8. Next assign students to small groups and distribute the Historical Evidence Form (Handout 9.3). Ask students to work with a partner within their group to re-read Malcolm X's speech and complete the inquiry form with information gained. Tell them that when they complete this first inquiry they should compare notes within their group. Let them know that each group will receive a second document to analyze in the same way.

9. Closely monitor students' understanding of the task, the questions, and any vocabulary words that may be challenging for them. Once you are confident that students have an understanding of what is expected, provide copies or website links to an additional document for research (Handout 9.4) to each group. Students should use the same inquiry questions to analyze their assigned document. If necessary, multiple groups may have the same documents.

10. Monitor groups as they complete their analysis of each document and provide them with appropriate feedback. Once groups have completed their analyses, display each docu-

ment using a projector or a poster size copy for the entire class to see. Ask groups to share the results of their analysis.

11. Distribute copies of Handout 9.5: Hear My Voice and ask groups to follow the directions to identify which quotes belong to Dr. Martin Luther King Jr. and which to Malcolm X. Allow time for students to complete their sorting and then ask for volunteers to identify the source for each quote, indicating a reason for their choice. Then tell students the correct responses (see Handout 9.6) so that they can resort their quotes if needed.

SOAR: SUMMARIZE, OBSERVE, ASSESS, REFLECT

12. Ask students to consider the two Civil Rights Movement leaders, Dr. King and Malcolm X, and share one way in which they were similar and one way in which they were different. You may want to remind students that they have already studied two leaders with similar goals but different methods for reaching those goals in the Post-Reconstruction unit: W. E. B. Du Bois and Booker T. Washington. Next, ask students to select one quote from either man that is particularly meaningful to them. Direct students to share these quotes and reasons within their small groups. Circulate among groups, listening for the connections students are able to make between the leaders' quotes and their own lives.

THINK AGAIN: HOMEWORK

13. Direct students to complete their analysis of the similarities and differences between the approaches to civil rights of Dr. King and Malcolm X by filling in Handout 9.7: Planning for Equal Rights: Goals, Messages, and Actions chart for Dr. King and Malcolm X.

KEEP ON GOING: LESSON EXTENSIONS

14. Encourage students to develop a profile of another leader in the Civil Rights Movement, someone who has not yet been mentioned in class. Ask the students to choose an original way of presenting information on this leader to stimulate interest from others in the class. Suggested persons are listed in Handout 9.8: People of the Civil Rights Movement.

HANDOUT 9.1
ESCALATION MODEL

ESCALATING CITIZEN ACTIONS

1. Do nothing. Think of your concerns.
2. Discuss your concerns with others.
3. Try to persuade others of your views.
4. Sign a petition.
5. Display concerns publicly, write letters.
6. Provide funds to organized protests.
7. Attend meetings, campaign.
8. Demonstrate, march, boycott, sit in.
9. Join an organized militant group.
10. Disobey laws and accept consequences for civil disobedience.

HANDOUT 9.2
MALCOLM X SPEECH: A MESSAGE TO THE GRASSROOTS

October 10, 1963

In this speech Malcolm X explains why the Black Revolution requires bloodshed. The following is an excerpt from this speech:

Look at the American Revolution, in 1776. That revolution was for what? For land. Why did they want land? Independence. How was it carried out? Bloodshed. Number one, it was based on land, the basis of independence. And the only way they could get it was bloodshed. The French Revolution—what was it based on? The landless against the landlord. What was it for? Land! How did they get it? Bloodshed! There was no love lost, was no compromise, was no negotiation. I'm telling you you don't know what a revolution is, because when you find out you'll get back in the alley; you'll get out of the way. The Russian Revolution. What was it based on? Land—the landless against the landlord. How did they bring it about? Bloodshed. You haven't got a revolution that doesn't involve bloodshed, and you're afraid to bleed. [Commotion] I said you are afraid to bleed. As long as the white man sent you to Korea, you bled. He sent you to Germany, you bled. He sent you to the South Pacific to fight the Japanese, you bled. You bleed for white people, but when it comes time to seeing your own churches being bombed, and little black girls [Speak on!] murdered, you haven't got no blood.

HANDOUT 9.3
HISTORICAL EVIDENCE FORM

Type of historical evidence: _____

Purpose: _____

Author: _____

Audience: _____

When: _____

What is the message?

_____

_____

_____

_____

_____

_____

_____

_____

_____

_____

_____

What does this evidence tell you about the author's beliefs?

_____

_____

_____

_____

_____

_____

_____

_____

_____

_____

_____

HANDOUT 9.4
RESEARCH ON MALCOLM X

Directions: Go to the Internet and locate the document assigned to your group. Review the document, using the questions from the Historical Evidence Form. Be prepared to share your findings, citing evidence from the document, to indicate what you discovered about Malcolm X in terms of his goals, general message, and suggested, planned, or completed actions.

> Document A: Letter From Malcolm X to Martin Luther King Jr. (includes sound clip): http://mlk-kpp01. stanford.edu/index.php/encyclopedia/documentsentry/letter_from_king_to_malcolm_x/

> Document B: Black Panther Party Poster: http://www.nyu.edu/library/bobst/collections/exhibits/arch/ 1969/1969-4.html

> Document C: Telegram From Malcolm X to Martin Luther King Jr., June 30, 1964: http://mlk-kpp01. stanford.edu/index.php/encyclopedia/documentsentry/telegram_from_malcolm_x/

> Document D: Malcolm X Speech at Harlem Rally, 1964: http://www.pbs.org/wgbh/amex/eyesontheprize/ sources/ps_noi.html

> Document E: Eulogy for Malcolm X Delivered by Ossie Davis: http://www.malcolmx.com/about/eulogy. html

HANDOUT 9.5
HEAR MY VOICE

Directions: In your small group, cut apart the quotations. Distribute the quotes among your group. Take turns reading your quote aloud and deciding together whether it belongs in the Dr. Martin Luther King Jr. pile or the Malcolm X pile. When you finish, compare your work with another group.

"We are nonviolent with people who are nonviolent with us."	"If you're not ready to die for it, put the word 'freedom' out of your vocabulary."	"The time is always right to do what's right."
"It is a time for martyrs now, and if I am to be one, it will be for the cause of brotherhood. That's the only thing that can save this country."	"Now is the time to rise from the dark and desolate valley of segregation to the sunlit path of racial justice."	"True peace is not merely the absence of tension: it is the presence of justice."
"Ultimately a genuine leader is not a searcher for consensus, but a molder of consensus."	"It is love that will save our world and our civilization, love even for enemies."	"Concerning nonviolence, it is criminal to teach a man not to defend himself when he is the constant victim of brutal attacks."
"I believe that there will ultimately be a clash between the oppressed and those that do the oppressing. I believe that there will be a clash between those who want freedom, justice and equality for everyone and those who want to continue the systems of exploitation."	"If violence is wrong in America, violence is wrong abroad. If it is wrong to be violent defending black women and black children and black babies and black men, then it is wrong for America to draft us, and make us violent abroad in defense of her. And if it is right for America to draft us, and teach us how to be violent in defense of her, then it is right for you and me to do whatever is necessary to defend our own people right here in this country."	"If you want to say that I was a drum major, say that I was a drum major for justice. Say that I was a drum major for peace. I was a drum major for righteousness."

HANDOUT 9.6
HEAR MY VOICE ANSWER KEY

DR. MARTIN LUTHER KING JR.

- ➤ "Now is the time to rise from the dark and desolate valley of segregation to the sunlit path of racial justice."
- ➤ "If you want to say that I was a drum major, say that I was a drum major for justice. Say that I was a drum major for peace. I was a drum major for righteousness."
- ➤ "Ultimately a genuine leader is not a searcher for consensus, but a molder of consensus."
- ➤ "It is love that will save our world and our civilization, love even for enemies."
- ➤ "The time is always right to do what's right."
- ➤ "True peace is not merely the absence of tension: it is the presence of justice."

Additional quotes are available at http://mlkday.gov/plan/library/communications/quotes.php

MALCOLM X

- ➤ "We are nonviolent with people who are nonviolent with us."
- ➤ "Concerning nonviolence, it is criminal to teach a man not to defend himself when he is the constant victim of brutal attacks."
- ➤ "If you're not ready to die for it, put the word 'freedom' out of your vocabulary."
- ➤ "I believe that there will ultimately be a clash between the oppressed and those that do the oppressing. I believe that there will be a clash between those who want freedom, justice and equality for everyone and those who want to continue the systems of exploitation."
- ➤ "It is a time for martyrs now, and if I am to be one, it will be for the cause of brotherhood. That's the only thing that can save this country."
- ➤ "If violence is wrong in America, violence is wrong abroad. If it is wrong to be violent defending black women and black children and black babies and black men, then it is wrong for America to draft us, and make us violent abroad in defense of her. And if it is right for America to draft us, and teach us how to be violent in defense of her, then it is right for you and me to do whatever is necessary to defend our own people right here in this country."

Additional quotes available at http://www.malcolmx.com/about/quotes.html

HANDOUT 9.7
PLANNING FOR EQUAL RIGHTS: GOALS, MESSAGES, ACTIONS

Directions: Complete the chart by describing one of each man's goals, messages, and actions.

	Dr. Martin Luther King Jr.	Malcolm X
Goals		
Messages (Quote)		
Actions		

HANDOUT 9.8
PEOPLE OF THE CIVIL RIGHTS MOVEMENT

Directions: Choose an original way to develop a profile of one of the following leaders in the Civil Rights Movement.

- ➤ Emmett Till
- ➤ Whitney M. Young
- ➤ Dorothy Height
- ➤ Bayard Rustin
- ➤ John Lewis
- ➤ Hosea Williams
- ➤ Gloria Richardson
- ➤ Philip Randolph
- ➤ Roy Wilkins
- ➤ James L. Farmer Jr.
- ➤ Thurgood Marshall
- ➤ Dwight D. Eisenhower
- ➤ Lyndon B. Johnson
- ➤ Earl Warren

LESSON 10
WHAT IS A MOVEMENT?

OVERVIEW

LESSON AT A GLANCE

➤ Students analyze descriptions of historic events to determine the essential elements of a movement.

➤ In a jigsaw format, students explore specific examples of movements including the Women's Movement and the American Indian Movement.

TIMELINE EVENTS

➤ 1848: First Women's Rights Convention
➤ 1869: National Women's Suffrage Association formed
➤ 1920: Nineteenth Amendment grants women the right to vote
➤ 1961: Commission on the Status of Women formed by President Kennedy
➤ 1963: Congress passes Equal Pay Act
➤ 1966: National Organization of Women (NOW) formed
➤ 1968: American Indian Movement (AIM) founded

ESSENTIAL QUESTIONS

➤ What makes something a movement?
➤ In what ways did societal and political changes in the 1950s and 1960s influence movements?
➤ In what ways do leaders bring about change?

CONCEPTUAL UNDERSTANDINGS

➤ The careful examination of historic events provides lessons for future social and political issues.
➤ Recognition of a person or group's perspective is critical to understanding their actions and effecting change.
➤ Equal rights refers to equality before the law for all. It is often used in reference to the fight for women's equality.
➤ Social justice movements seek to facilitate equal opportunity for everyone to lead a fulfilling life and be active contributors to their community.

IMPORTANT TERMS AND IDEAS

➤ *platform*: public statements of beliefs and goals, usually by a candidate or political party
➤ *civil liberties*: rights of citizens guaranteed by the Bill of Rights
➤ *suffrage*: the right to vote
➤ *tension*: intensity, stress, strain
➤ *feminism*: advocating equal social, political, and economic rights for women

MATERIALS

➤ Handout 10.1: Read-Aloud Excerpt From *The Feminine Mystique*
➤ Handout 10.2: Movements Chart
➤ Handout 10.3: Equal Pay for Women, Please
➤ Handout 10.4: Title IX: It's Not Just About Sports!
➤ Handout 10.5: The Mercury 13: Training U.S. Women for Space
➤ Handout 10.6: The American Indians and Civil Rights
➤ Handout 10.7: A Brief History of the American Indian Movement

SUGGESTED RESOURCES

➤ http://lcweb2.loc.gov/ammem/awhhtml/
➤ http://digital.mtsu.edu/cdm/landingpage/collection/women
➤ http://www.smith.edu/libraries/libs/ssc/
➤ http://www.nwhp.org/
➤ http://www.womenshistorymonth.gov/profiles/susanbanthony.html
➤ http://www.aimovement.org/
➤ Alexie, S. (2009). *The absolutely true diary of a part-time Indian.* New York, NY: Little, Brown.
➤ Carlson, L. (1995). *American eyes.* New York, NY: Random House.
➤ Ochoa, A., Franco, B., & Gourdine, T. (Eds.). (2003). *Night is gone, day is still coming.* New York, NY: Candlewick Press.
➤ Yang, G. (2008). *American born Chinese.* New York, NY: First Second.

INSTRUCTIONS

THE HOOK

1. Ask students how they think life might be different for women today than it was in the 1960s. Read students the excerpt from Betty Friedan's *The Feminine Mystique* (Handout 10.1). Allow students time to react and comment. Ask if anyone knows what the Women's Movement of the 1960s and 1970s involved. What issues? Ask if they remember Thurgood Marshall from earlier lessons. A civil rights lawyer, Thurgood Marshall was the first African American justice to sit on the Supreme Court. He was also on the team of lawyers who argued *Brown v. Board of Education*. Explain that in 1963, Betty Friedan's book was a clas-

sic work that helped define issues related to women's liberation. Were the magazine editor's comments surprising?

DEVELOPING CONCEPTUAL UNDERSTANDING

2. Tell students: *Everyone has some things that really bother them to the point where they think others are infringing on their rights. For example, I am bothered by people who talk on cell phones in restaurants and disturb my meal. It also bothers me when people use bad language in public. Think about issues you may have with someone or a group of people. After you have had a few minutes to come up with an idea, I will ask you to share with a partner and then we will ask some of you to share with the class.* Allow think time and then ask students to discuss with a partner. Finally, ask for a few examples from the class and determine whether or not several people have the same issues.

3. Help students gain an understanding of the concept of a social movement by analyzing examples of group actions. First, share with them the views of Charles Tilly, a noted American social scientist, associated with social movements. (See teacher's note for details.) Tell students that social scientists define their terms so that there is agreement about things. Charles Tilly suggested that movements are defined by their worthiness, unity, numbers, and commitment. Thus, the acronym WUNC was formed.

> ***Teacher's Note.*** Charles Tilly (2004) argued that social movements combine:
> 1. A sustained, organized public effort making collective claims on target audiences: let us call it a campaign.
> 2. Employment of combinations from among the following forms of political action: creation of special purpose associations and coalitions, public meetings, solemn processions, vigils, rallies, demonstrations, petition drives, statements to and in public media, and pamphleteering; call the variable ensemble of performances the social movement repertoire.
> 3. Participants' concerted public representations of worthiness, unity, numbers and commitment (WUNC) on the part of themselves and/or their constituencies. (p. 53)

4. Next, ask students to comment on which elements of a movement are present and which are not in the following examples:
   - A series of marches is held in cities across the country by disabled persons seeking a higher quality of life and nondiscrimination.
   - A group of college students gathers in front of the football field with signs and posters to support their team as the rival team gets off their bus.
   - A Facebook page is earmarked for commentary about unfair cuts in school spending in your town. Hundreds of people visit the page and make comments. Someone copies the comments to send to the school board.
   - A woman sits in a giant 180-foot Redwood tree in California for 738 days to spare the tree.

- A group of farmers band together to form an organization. They have social events and eventually present a strong, vocal, and united front in support of fair pricing and fair treatment by banks and companies as well as legislative assistance.
- The animal advocacy group PETA got a state law amended that had previously required government animal shelters to sell dogs and cats to university laboratories for use in cruel experiments. The group had released their findings from an undercover investigation of the cruel use of the animals.

5. Next, ask students to put into their own words their ideas about the essential elements of a movement. If needed, prompt them with ideas such as size, scope, issues, and united front. Record their ideas on chart paper. You may want to use a concept development graphic to guide the discussion, similar to those used in Lesson 5.

6. Tell students that today they will learn about different movements that were influenced by the Civil Rights Movement, including women's rights and American Indian rights. Let them know that these are two examples of movements that gained momentum during the 1950s and 1960s. Divide students into five equal groups. Give each group one handout (10.3–10.7) to examine. Direct students to complete the sections of the movements chart in Handout 10.2 for their assigned topic. Let students know that when every group has finished its part of the chart, the groups will split up in jigsaw fashion, so that one member of each original group shares its information with a new group. Thus, in the second round, groups will have one person from each topic ready to share what they learned from reading the assigned documents. Suggest that they take careful notes so that each of them will be able to share the information with others who did not read their article.

7. **Jigsaw activity.** Allow students time to complete their work (approximately 15 minutes). Reorganize the groups so that one student from each original group is now in a new group with one person from each of the other groups. This arrangement should allow for each student in the new group to be an "expert" on his or her initial topic. Direct students to share what they learned while others in the jigsaw group take notes on their presentation. By the end of this jigsaw activity, students should have completed the entire movements chart.

SOAR: SUMMARIZE, OBSERVE, ASSESS, REFLECT

8. Ask students: *What makes something a movement?* Be sure students mention the elements of a movement discussed earlier in the lesson (worthiness, unity, numbers, and commitment). Then discuss ways in which what they talked about in their groups could have been part of the Women's Movement or the American Indian Movement. Tell students that these movements occurred because a number of people so believed in a certain social and/or political issue that they began to form and organize and present their issue in a way that sustained their efforts over time. Ask students to help you make a class list of current social issues that are important to them. By show of hands, determine the five most popular issues. Tell students that tomorrow's lesson will offer them an opportunity to discuss their selected issue, to complete some research on the issue, and to prepare representations of their ideas for supporting a movement related to the issue.

Tell them that their thinking about these ideas will be preparation for their group work in class.

THINK AGAIN: HOMEWORK

9. Ask students to talk about movements and protests at home, asking if anyone in the family can give an example of a movement or a protest. If a newspaper is available, they can scan the paper for additional examples. Ask them to be prepared to share one idea in the next class.

KEEP ON GOING: LESSON EXTENSIONS

10. Ask students to visit websites of some advocacy groups to determine current efforts of these organizations. Suggested groups include:
    - Equal Rights Advocates
    - National Association for the Advancement of Colored People (NAACP)
    - National Fair Housing Alliance
    - Center for Media Justice
    - National Congress of American Indians
    - National Council of Negro Women
    - Japanese American Citizens League
    - Organization of Chinese Americans
    - National Council of La Raza
    - National Immigration Law Center

Additional top-rated nonprofit social justice groups can be found at: http://greatnonprofits. org/issues/social-justice.

HANDOUT 10.1
READ-ALOUD EXCERPT FROM THE FEMININE MYSTIQUE

I sat one night at a meeting of magazine writers, mostly men, who work for all kinds of magazines, including women's magazines. The main speaker was a leader of the desegregation battle. Before he spoke, another man outlined the needs of the large women's magazine he edited:

> Our readers are housewives, full time. They're not interested in the broad public issues of the day. They are not interested in national or international affairs. They are only interested in family and the home. They aren't interested in politics, unless it's related to an immediate need in the home, like the price of coffee. Humor? Has to be gentle, they don't get satire. Travel? We have almost completely dropped it. Education? That's a problem. Their own education level is going up. They've generally all had a high-school education and many, college. They're tremendously interested in education for their children—fourth-grade arithmetic. You just can't write about ideas or broad issues of the day for women. That's why we're publishing 90 per cent service now and 10 per cent general interest.

Another editor agreed, adding plaintively: "Can't you give us something else besides 'there's death in your medicine cabinet?' Can't any of you dream up a new crisis for women? We're always interested in sex, of course."

At this point, the writers and editors spent an hour listening to Thurgood Marshall on the inside story of the desegregation battle, and its possible effects on the presidential election. "Too bad I can't run that story," one editor said. "But you just can't link it to woman's world."

Note. Excerpt from *The Feminine Mystique* (p. 84) by B. Friedan, 1963.

HANDOUT 10.2
MOVEMENTS CHART

Topic	Who Is Involved?	Issue or Concern	Action Taken	Outcome
NASA				
Equal Pay for Women				
Title IX				
AIM				
American Indian Civil Rights				

HANDOUT 10.3
EQUAL PAY FOR WOMEN, PLEASE

KEY EVENTS IN THE QUEST FOR EQUAL PAY

1932: Wives of federal employees were banned from holding government positions by legislative act. Women whose husbands were employed were first on the list of people to be fired.

1935: Women in government jobs received 25% less than men in the same jobs, ordered by the National Recovery Act.

1942: The War Labor Board ruled in favor of women receiving the same pay for jobs formerly done by men gone to war but this rule was never enforced because the end of the war made it unnecessary. At the end of the war, most women lost their jobs to make room for returning veterans.

1950s: Although some bills were introduced for equal pay, they were not acted upon. Newspaper ads published job openings in separate categories for men and women. Listed under "Help Wanted—Female" were lower level jobs, with the higher level ones listed under "Help Wanted—Male." Pay for women's jobs, even those with the same requirements and duties, were often substantially less.

1961: Another equal pay bill was introduced with evidence gathered through the head of the Women's Bureau, Ester Peterson, a labor activist. Around this time, women were making 54–60 cents for every dollar earned by men.

1963: The Equal Pay Act was passed, providing equal pay for women for equal work.

1964: The Civil Rights Act passes and Title VII bans employment discrimination against women in hiring, wages, assignment, promotions, benefits, discipline, discharge, layoffs, and almost every aspect of employment.

1970s: Two landmark court cases supported the intent of the Civil Rights Act in terms of equal pay.

➤ *Schultz v. Wheaton Glass Co.* ruled that an employer cannot change the title of a job to pay less to a woman. Jobs that are substantially equal are protected under the Equal Pay Act.

➤ *Corning Glass Works v. Brennan* ruled that "the going market rate" for women cannot be used to justify lower wages for women.

WHERE ARE WE TODAY?

According to the White House website on equal pay for women:

> Despite passage of the Equal Pay Act of 1963, which requires that men and women in the same work place be given equal pay for equal work, the "gender gap" in pay persists. Full-time women workers' earnings are only about 77 percent of their male counterparts' earnings. The pay gap is even greater for African-American and Latina women, with African-American women earning 64 cents and Latina women earning 56 cents for every dollar earned by a Caucasian man. Decades of research shows that no matter how you evaluate the data, there remains a pay gap—even after factoring in the kind of work people do, or qualifications such as education and experience—and there is good evidence that discrimination contributes to the persistent pay disparity between men and women. (para. 2)

The Lilly Ledbetter Fair Pay Act was signed into law in 2009, but the struggle to gain equal pay for women continues.

HANDOUT 10.4
TITLE IX: IT'S NOT JUST ABOUT SPORTS!

	Before Title IX	After Title IX
Access to Higher Education	Colleges and universities refused to admit women. Women were considered to be more concerned with marriage and children.	Women now earn undergraduate and graduate degrees at a much higher rate and unfair admissions and financial aid practices are rare. Women are also going into some fields that were traditionally dominated by men, such as engineering, medicine, and law.
Athletics	Cheerleading and square-dancing were the primary physical activities for girls. There also were virtually no college scholarships for female athletes, however when they did receive money, it was only 2% of the overall budget!	There are more opportunities to participate in sports and receive scholarships in college, as well as compete at elite levels such as the Olympics, World Championships, and professional leagues.
Career Education and Math and Science	Women were primarily trained for low-wage, traditionally female jobs like health aides, nurses, teachers, or cosmetologists. It was assumed that girls didn't like math and science and therefore weren't good at those subjects.	Today girls and women are free to pursue career training in courses like aviation, automotive repair, and architectural drafting. Career training is by choice, not gender. In addition, girls are now taking upper level math and science courses required for math and science majors in college.
Employment	Women mainly taught in the elementary or secondary schools, while men primarily taught at the college or university level. Very few women were hired in high-level administrative positions throughout colleges and universities.	A much higher number of female faculty members are being hired. The women professors are making more money, however the male professors continue to make more money than the female professors. Some women are now holding jobs in the top administrative positions.
Standardized Testing	Girls consistently scored lower on standardized tests than boys. There was no consideration to how the questions were asked, the kinds of questions that were asked, or that gender influenced the test scores.	Now all standardized tests must be valid predictors of success in the areas being tested and they must measure what they say they are measuring. The tests must be reliable or they are considered unlawful!

HANDOUT 10.5
THE MERCURY 13: TRAINING U.S. WOMEN FOR SPACE

LOVELACE'S WOMAN IN SPACE PROGRAM

Lovelace's Woman in Space Program was a short-lived, privately-funded project testing women pilots for astronaut fitness in the early 1960s. Although nothing concrete resulted, the women who participated have since been recognized as trailblazers, whose ambitions to fly the newest and the fastest craft led them to be among the first American women to gain access to sophisticated aerospace medical tests.

The Woman in Space Program began as an Air Force project that grew out of two researchers' interests in women's capabilities for spaceflight. Because, on the average, women are smaller and lighter than men are, scientists speculated that they might make good occupants for cramped space vehicles. In 1960, Dr. William Randolph "Randy" Lovelace II and Brig. General Donald Flickinger invited award-winning pilot Geraldyn "Jerrie" Cobb to undergo the physical testing regimen that Lovelace's Albuquerque, New Mexico Foundation had developed to help select NASA's first astronauts. Although the Lovelace Foundation for Medical Education and Research was a private organization, Dr. Lovelace also served as head of NASA's Special Committee on Bioastronautics. When Cobb became the first woman to pass those tests, Lovelace announced her success at a 1960 conference in Stockholm, Sweden. As Cobb coped with the ensuing publicity, Lovelace invited more women pilots to take the tests. Jacqueline Cochran, the famous pilot, businesswoman, and Lovelace's old friend, joined the project as an advisor and paid all of the women's testing expenses.

By the end of the summer of 1961, nineteen women pilots had taken astronaut fitness examinations at the Lovelace Clinic. Unlike NASA's male candidates, who competed in group, each woman came to Albuquerque either alone or in a pair for the week of tests. All of the women were skilled airplane pilots with commercial ratings. Most of them were recruited through the Ninety-Nines, a women pilot's organization. Others heard about the testing through friends or newspaper articles and volunteered. The oldest candidate, Jane Hart, was a forty-one year old mother of eight and the wife of a U.S. Senator (Philip Hart-D of Michigan). The youngest, Wally Funk, was a twenty-three year old flight instructor.

Since no human being had flown in space yet when the astronaut fitness tests were designed, the Lovelace doctors required very thorough examinations. These included numerous X-rays and a four-hour eye exam. A specially weighted stationary bicycle pushed the women to exhaustion while testing their respiration. The doctors had the women swallow a rubber tube so that they could test their stomach acids. A tilt table tested circulation. Using an electrical pulse, the physicians tested nerve reflexes in their arms. Ice water was shot into the women's ears to induce vertigo so that the doctors could time how quickly they recovered. They calculated the candidates' lean body mass using a nuclear counter in Los Alamos. By the end of the week, the women had no secrets from the Lovelace physicians.

In the end, thirteen women passed the same physical examinations that the Lovelace Foundation had developed for NASA's astronaut selection process. Those thirteen women were:

- ➤ Jerrie Cobb
- ➤ Wally Funk
- ➤ Irene Leverton
- ➤ Myrtle "K" Cagle
- ➤ Jane B. Hart
- ➤ Gene Nora Stumbough [Jessen]
- ➤ Jerri Sloan [Truhill]

- ➤ Rhea Hurrle [Woltman]
- ➤ Sarah Gorelick [Ratley]
- ➤ Bernice "B" Trimble Steadman
- ➤ Jan Dietrich
- ➤ Marion Dietrich (now deceased)
- ➤ Jean Hixson (now deceased)

Handout 10.5: The Mercury 13: Training U.S. Women for Space, continued

A few women took additional tests. Jerrie Cobb, Rhea Hurrle, and Wally Funk went to Oklahoma City for an isolation tank test and psychological evaluations. Because of other family and job commitments, not all of the women were asked to take these tests, however. Instead, the group prepared to gather in Pensacola, Florida at the Naval School of Aviation Medicine to undergo advanced aeromedical examinations using military equipment and jet aircraft. Two of the women quit their jobs in order to be able to attend. A few days before they were to report, however, the women received telegrams abruptly canceling the Pensacola testing. Without an official NASA request to run the tests, the Navy would not allow the use of their facilities for an unofficial project.

Jerrie Cobb immediately flew to Washington, D.C. to try to have the testing program resumed. She and Jane Hart wrote to President John Kennedy and visited Vice President Lyndon Johnson. Finally, on the 17th and 18th of July 1962, Representative Victor Anfuso (R) of New York convened public hearings before a special Subcommittee of the House Committee on Science and Astronautics. Significantly, the hearings investigated sex discrimination two full years before the 1964 Civil Rights Act made that illegal, making these hearings a marker of how ideas about women's rights permeated political discourse even before they were enshrined in law. Cobb and Hart testified about the benefits of Lovelace's private project. Jackie Cochran talked about her concerns that setting up a special program to train a woman astronaut could hurt the space program. NASA representatives George Low and Astronauts John Glenn and Scott Carpenter testified that the women could not qualify as astronaut candidates. NASA required all astronauts to be graduates of military jet test piloting programs and have engineering degrees. In 1962, no women could meet these requirements. Although the Subcommittee was sympathetic to the women's arguments, no action resulted.

Lovelace's privately-funded women's testing project received renewed media attention when Soviet cosmonaut Valentina Tereshkova became the first woman in space in 1963. In response, Clare Booth Luce published an article in Life magazine criticizing NASA and American decision makers. By including photographs of all thirteen Lovelace finalists, the names of all thirteen women became public for the first time. (Significant media coverage had already spotlighted some of the participants, however.)

Although both Cobb and Cochran made separate appeals for years afterward to restart a women's astronaut testing project, the U.S. civil space agency did not select any female astronaut candidates until the 1978 class of Space Shuttle astronauts. Astronaut Sally Ride became the first American woman in space in 1983 on STS-7, and Eileen Collins was the first woman to pilot the Space Shuttle during STS-63 in 1995. Collins also became the first woman to command a Space Shuttle mission during STS-93 in 1999. In 2005, she commanded NASA's return to flight mission, STS-114. At Collins' invitation, eight of the eleven surviving Lovelace finalists attended her first launch and she has flown mementos for almost all of them. The women of Lovelace's Woman in Space Program feel a special kinship with Collins, who in the 1990s finally fulfilled their thirty-year dream of seeing an American woman *pilot* astronaut.

Note. From "Lovelace's Woman in Space Program" by Margaret A. Weitekamp, 2010. Reprinted courtesy of National Aeronautics and Space Administration History Program Office.

HANDOUT 10.6
THE AMERICAN INDIANS AND CIVIL RIGHTS

Topic	Issues
Dual Citizenship	Native Americans' unique situation gives them citizenship rights both as members of tribes and as citizens of the states in which they reside and of the United States. Within the tribal organization and before the tribal courts, their rights are vague and undefined. Chairman Ervin of the Subcommittee on Constitutional Rights of the U.S. Senate has said, " . . . it appears that a tribe can deprive its members of property and liberty without due process of law." So, Native Americans have freedom of religion, speech and press, are protected against unlawful search, seizure, self-incrimination, cruel and unusual punishment, and are assured representation by counsel and equal protection of the law as citizens of the states in which they reside and of the United States. However, within their tribal organization and before the tribal courts, these same rights and protections do not apply.
Unemployment	Indian unemployment is 7 or 8 times the national average. Some Native American communities are economically depressed with few large businesses or other industry that would provide jobs for people.
Land	Although Native Americans collectively, and in some cases individually, own large parcels of land set aside in reservations, they are not free to dispose of the land. The land is held in trust by the U.S. Government. In 1887, the U.S. government began a program to "de-tribal-ize" the Indian population and granted allotments of land to individual Indians. The Native Americans did have control over this land and were permitted to sell the land as they saw fit. However, with their limited knowledge, some Native Americans sold their land for little or nothing.
Language	Many of the Native American leaders do not speak English and have very little education. This causes a large problem when communicating with witnesses within the tribal courts.
Schools and Libraries	Access to schools and public libraries was limited to Native Americans, leaving many of them with very limited formal education.
Medical	The Native Americans are the only group within the U.S. that receives medial care provided through the Public Health Service. A full range of federal hospital and outpatient clinical services are also provide through the U.S. Public Health Service.
Voting Rights	Native Americans do have the right to vote, however they have played a very small role. There has never been an attempt to prevent them from voting, however with the language barriers and being somewhat isolated from society, they have played a small role in the election process.

HANDOUT 10.7
A BRIEF HISTORY OF THE AMERICAN INDIAN MOVEMENT

A BRIEF HISTORY OF THE AMERICAN INDIAN MOVEMENT
by Laura Waterman Wittstock and Elaine J. Salinas

In the 30 years of its formal history, the American Indian Movement (AIM) has given witness to a great many changes. We say formal history, because the movement existed for 500 years without a name. The leaders and members of today's AIM never fail to remember all of those who have traveled on before, having given their talent and their lives for the survival of the people.

At the core of the movement is Indian leadership under the direction of NeeGawNwayWeeDun, Clyde H. Bellecourt, and others. Making steady progress, the movement has transformed policy making into programs and organizations that have served Indian people in many communities. These policies have consistently been made in consultation with spiritual leaders and elders. The success of these efforts is indisputable, but perhaps even greater than the accomplishments is the vision defining what AIM stands for.

Indian people were never intended to survive the settlement of Europeans in the Western Hemisphere, our Turtle Island. With the strength of a spiritual base, AIM has been able to clearly articulate the claims of Native Nations and has had the will and intellect to put forth those claims.

The movement was founded to turn the attention of Indian people toward a renewal of spirituality which would impart the strength of resolve needed to reverse the ruinous policies of the United States, Canada, and other colonialist governments of Central and South America. At the heart of AIM is deep spirituality and a belief in the connectedness of all Indian people.

During the past thirty years, The American Indian Movement has organized communities and created opportunities for people across the Americas and Canada. AIM is headquartered in Minneapolis with chapters in many other cities, rural areas and Indian Nations.

AIM has repeatedly brought successful suit against the federal government for the protection of the rights of Native Nations guaranteed in treaties, sovereignty, the United States Constitution, and laws. The philosophy of self-determination upon which the movement is built is deeply rooted in traditional spirituality, culture, language and history. AIM develops partnerships to address the common needs of the people. Its first mandate is to ensure the fulfillment of treaties made with the United States. This is the clear and unwavering vision of The American Indian Movement.

It has not been an easy path. Spiritual leaders and elders foresaw the testing of AIM's strength and stamina. Doubters, infiltrators, those who wished they were in the leadership, and those who didn't want to be but wanted to tear down and take away have had their turns. No one, inside or outside the movement, has so far been able to destroy the will and strength of AIM's solidarity. Men and women, adults and children are continuously urged to stay strong spiritually, and to always remember that the movement is greater than the accomplishments or faults of its leaders.

Inherent in the spiritual heart of AIM is knowing that the work goes on because the need goes on.

Indian people live on Mother Earth with the clear understanding that no one will assure the coming generations except ourselves. No one from the outside will do this for us. And no person among us can do it all for us, either. Self-determination must be the goal of all work. Solidarity must be the first and only defense of the members.

Handout 10.7: A Brief History of the American Indian Movement, continued

In November, 1972 AIM brought a caravan of Native Nation representatives to Washington, DC, to the place where dealings with Indians have taken place since 1849: the US Department of Interior. AIM put the following claims directly before the President of the United States:

1. Restoration of treaty making (ended by Congress in 1871).
2. Establishment of a treaty commission to make new treaties (with sovereign Native Nations).
3. Indian leaders to address Congress.
4. Review of treaty commitments and violations.
5. Unratified treaties to go before the Senate.
6. All Indians to be governed by treaty relations.
7. Relief for Native Nations for treaty rights violations.
8. Recognition of the right of Indians to interpret treaties.
9. Joint Congressional Committee to be formed on reconstruction of Indian relations.
10. Restoration of 110 million acres of land taken away from Native Nations by the United States.
11. Restoration of terminated rights.
12. Repeal of state jurisdiction on Native Nations.
13. Federal protection for offenses against Indians.
14. Abolishment of the Bureau of Indian Affairs.
15. Creation of a new office of Federal Indian Relations.
16. New office to remedy breakdown in the constitutionally prescribed relationships between the United States and Native Nations.
17. Native Nations to be immune to commerce regulation, taxes, trade restrictions of states.
18. Indian religious freedom and cultural integrity protected.
19. Establishment of national Indian voting with local options; free national Indian organizations from governmental controls
20. Reclaim and affirm health, housing, employment, economic development, and education for all Indian people.

(*The Preamble and complete text of the Trail of Broken Treaties 20-Point Indian Manifesto.*)

These twenty points, twenty-six years later, state clearly what has to happen if there is to be protection of Native rights, and a future free from the dictates of the country that surrounds the Native Nations. These claims clearly reaffirm that Indian people are sovereign people. Despite the history and the accomplishments, AIM is difficult to identify for some people. It seems to stand for many things at once—the protection of treaty rights and the preservation of spirituality and culture. But what else? Unlike the American civil rights movement, with which it has been compared, AIM has seen self-determination and racism differently. Desegregation was not a goal. Individual rights were not placed ahead of the preservation of Native Nation sovereignty. At the 1971 AIM national conference it was decided that translating policy to practice meant building organizations—schools and housing and employment services. In Minnesota, AIM's birthplace, that is exactly what was done.

Over the years, as the organizations have grown, they have continued to serve the community from a base of Indian culture. Before AIM in 1968, culture had been weakened in most Indian communities due to U.S. policy, the American boarding schools and all the other efforts to extinguish Indian secular and spiritual life. Now, many groups cannot remember a time without culture. This great revival has also helped to restore spiritual leaders and elders to their former positions of esteem for the wisdom and the history they hold.

All of these actions are in concert with the principles of AIM and came into being at this time in history because Indian people have refused to relinquish their sovereign right to exist as a free and uncolonized people.

Note. Reprinted with permission from http://www.aimovement.org/ggc/history.html.

LESSON 11
WHO WORKS FOR SOCIAL JUSTICE?

OVERVIEW

LESSON AT A GLANCE

➤ Students work in small groups to select a contemporary social justice issue.
➤ Student groups complete research on their selected social justice issue and identify key points.
➤ Students develop a format for presenting their cause to the class audience.

TIMELINE EVENTS

➤ 1960s: Civil Rights Movement
➤ 1960s: Women's Movement
➤ 1960s: Anti-War Movement
➤ 1960s: LBGT Movement
➤ 1960s: Environmental Movement
➤ 1970s: Disability Rights Movement
➤ 1990s: Global Rights Movement

ESSENTIAL QUESTIONS

➤ What makes something a movement?
➤ In what ways did societal and political changes in the 1950s and 1960s influence movements?
➤ In what ways are movements a reflection of ordinary people's participation in politics?
➤ In what ways do leaders bring about change?

CONCEPTUAL UNDERSTANDINGS

➤ Human injustices have been seen throughout history as the result of discrimination against race, religion, gender, or economic status.
➤ Contemporary movements often build upon the tactics and successes of the Civil Rights Movement.

IMPORTANT TERMS AND CONCEPTS

➤ *disability*: physical or mental challenge
➤ *LBGT*: lesbian, bisexual, gay, transgender
➤ *injustice*: an unfair or illegal act
➤ *discrimination*: unfair treatment based on a certain characteristic, usually race, religion, or gender
➤ *contemporary*: of the current times

MATERIALS

➤ Handout 11.1: What Makes a Movement?
➤ Poster board and markers
➤ Access to Internet

SUGGESTED RESOURCES

➤ Amnesty International. (Ed.). (2010). *Free? Stories about human rights.* Somerville, MA: Candlewick.
➤ Singer, J. (2006). *Stirring up justice: Writing and reading to change the world.* Portsmouth, NH: Heinemann.
➤ Sundem, G. (2010). *Real kids, real stories, real change: Courageous actions around the world.* Minneapolis, MN: Free Spirit.
➤ Wilson, J. (2013). *Our rights: How kids are changing the world.* Toronto, ON: Second Story Press.

INSTRUCTIONS

THE HOOK

1. Display the class list of issues selected in the previous lesson as five signs located in different parts of the classroom (clusters of desks, tables). Ask students to join one of the groups. Work with the students to even out the groups to some extent. Be sure each student feels some level of commitment to his or her group's issue. If necessary, allow groups to be of different sizes. Ask each group to make a list of words and phrases that come to their mind when they think of the social justice issue they have selected and display their list. Review the groups' lists and comment on similarities and differences.

DEVELOPING CONCEPTUAL UNDERSTANDING

2. Tell students that the remainder of this class period will be devoted to their group work on a social justice plan that includes the three dimensions of a movement:
   a. A sustained effort toward a target audience (a campaign)
   b. A combination of forms of political action
   c. Public representations of worthiness, unity, numbers, and commitment

3. Distribute Handout 11.1 and ask groups to discuss these components for the makings of a movement in relation to their social justice cause. Allow a few minutes for students to think about what each of these mean in relation to their social justice efforts. When students express understanding of the need for developing a plan that incorporates all three, suggest that each group begin its work in terms of research and an action plan.

4. Ask students to consider what is realistic yet powerful in terms of advocating for change, assuming their efforts will be student-led and guided. Remind them that their efforts must be ones they can tackle and that at the end of the class they will present their plans to the entire class for consideration. Also ask students to consider what they, as individuals, might have as an idea for responding to injustice in a way that might influence others to become advocates for their cause.

5. Suggest to students that they consider some of the ways in which nonviolent actions were effective during the civil rights movements of the past and which types of efforts are popular today in presenting messages to a wider audience (news clips, public speaking, documentaries, posters, blogs, webpages, Twitter, etc.) Make a list of these ideas with the students.

6. Allow time for students to research their cause and develop their group action plan. Remind them that they need to present their work with a focus on the condition or policy or practice that has resulted in unfairness or inequity and ways in which they might advocate for change, specifying the change they hope to see.

SOAR: SUMMARIZE, ASSESS, OBSERVE, REFLECT

7. As students complete their presentations, ask them to record a reflection statement on each presentation and allow for some sharing of these comments. Assess students' understanding of the components of a movement, the development of a collective identity, and the match of efforts to perceived results in their action plans. Summarize presentations and ask students to consider whether or not as a class they would like to "adopt" one of these efforts to pursue further. You may choose to what degree you wish to guide students in continuing these efforts.

THINK AGAIN: HOMEWORK

8. Ask students to use the idea for a social justice effort they developed in class and create something that might be used in the campaign (signs, posters, art, songs, poems, role plays, or stories).

KEEP ON GOING: LESSON EXTENSIONS

9. Invite students to keep a record of their planning and actions to develop a story about their social justice issue and ideas for moving forward to make progress toward a goal or their actual activities. Identify places for such a story to be published, such as the class or school newspaper, newsletter, faculty bulletin, community connections, or an appropriate online site.

HANDOUT 11.1
WHAT MAKES A MOVEMENT?

What Makes a Movement?	
The Key Issue	
Current Conditions	
Proposed Solution/s or Resolution	
Action Plans	

LESSON 12
WHAT HAVE WE LEARNED ABOUT THE CIVIL RIGHTS MOVEMENT?

OVERVIEW

SESSION AT A GLANCE

➤ Students share stories, poems, and personal ideas about social, economic, or political social justice issues worthy of attention.

➤ Students reflect on what they have learned and demonstrate their progress through a postassessment.

TIMELINE EVENTS

➤ 1954–1965: Era of Civil Rights Movement

ESSENTIAL QUESTIONS

➤ What is the lasting impact of the Civil Rights Movement?

➤ How has the idea of democratic citizenship changed since the end of the Civil Rights Movement?

➤ Has the quest for equal rights been realized?

CONCEPTUAL UNDERSTANDINGS

➤ The Civil Rights Movement was a continuation of the quest for African Americans' equal rights.

➤ Leadership in the Civil Rights Movement came from individuals young and old; school, church, and community groups; organizations; nationally prominent people; and judges, legislators, and presidents.

➤ The Civil Rights Movement resulted in greater rights and equality for all Americans.

➤ Other groups who experienced oppression led other movements for equality including women and American Indians.

➤ The struggle for equal rights did not end with the Civil Rights Movement; it continues to the present day.

➤ Social justice movements continue the work of the Civil Rights Movement.

IMPORTANT TERMS AND IDEAS

> ➤ *resolution*: the resulting state
> ➤ *oppression*: state of being heavily burdened by poor conditions or abuse

MATERIALS

> ➤ A copy of the lyrics to Bob Dylan's "The Times They Are a-Changin'" and the audio track to this song (http://www.bobdylan.com/us/songs/times-they-are-changin)
> ➤ Charts completed in Lesson 1
> ➤ Documents used in Lesson 1
> ➤ 4 x 6 index cards
> ➤ Handout 12.1: Civil Rights Movement Postassessment

SUGGESTED RESOURCES

> ➤ *Let Freedom Ring: Moments From the Civil Rights Movement* DVD (Films Media group, 2009, 47 minutes). Narrated by Lester Holt, this NBC documentary recounts the *Brown v. Board of Education* decision, the Montgomery Bus Boycott, the integration of Little Rock High School, the Nashville lunch counter sit-ins, Freedom Rides, The March on Washington, and Freedom Summer.

INSTRUCTIONS

Prior to the start of the lesson, you may want to play some music of the era in the background. Display the graffiti wall students created in Lesson 1.

THE HOOK

1. Begin this session by playing Bob Dylan's "The Times They Are a-Changin.'" Display the lyrics and/or provide students with copies. Ask students to reflect on the lyrics and suggest in what ways they see this song as reflective of the Civil Rights Movement.

2. Ask students: *It is said that the Civil Rights Movement was important for all Americans. Do you agree with this statement? In what ways do you think the Civil Rights Movement impacted your life? Is the election of President Obama a reflection of the impact of the Civil Rights Movement? Why or why not? What are some of the lasting results of the Civil Rights Movement?*

DEVELOPING CONCEPTUAL UNDERSTANDING

3. Give each student an index card on which to record his or her response to the question: *What is one thing you now know that you did not know at the beginning of this unit on civil rights?* Allow students a few minutes to record their statements. Collect their cards and read several of their responses aloud, encouraging commentary about things they

recorded. Remind students of the day they began this unit and the things they recorded as their prior knowledge. Tell students that today is an opportunity to revisit those same questions and record more of what they know now as a result of their participation in the unit.

4. Distribute copies of the postassessment (Handout 12.1) and ask students to work alone to complete it. Let them know that, just as you did with the preassessment, you will be giving them general feedback about how well the class has demonstrated its knowledge. You may choose to provide students with their preassessments after they have completed the postassessment to enable them to recognize the progress they have made. Offer feedback to the group a day or two after the conclusion of the unit to let them know your overall impressions of their new knowledge and understanding as reflected in the postassessment.

5. After students have completed the postassessment, invite student social justice groups to share their signs, posters, songs, poems, art, role-plays, or stories completed in the prior lesson. These products represent their personal thoughts, beliefs, and values related to the Civil Rights Movement. Encourage student groups to display their reflections in an appropriate place in the classroom and/or online in a class wiki or on a webpage and ask students to discuss their thoughts about extending their activities related to the particular social justice cause they have presented.

SOAR: SUMMARIZE, OBSERVE, ASSESS, REFLECT

6. Show students some or all of the DVD *Let Freedom Ring*. At the conclusion of the video, ask students to reflect on the images and the emotions of individuals and groups who lived through this period in history. Ask students to volunteer to share one "life lesson" they learned from this study. Conclude the unit with a discussion of democratic citizenship and what it means to the students. Ask them to share ideas for their own future in terms of ways in which they hope to impact society for the better.

HANDOUT 12.1
CIVIL RIGHTS MOVEMENT
POSTASSESSMENT

1. Think of individuals, groups, or events that made significant contributions to the Civil Rights Movement. Record what you know for each one you choose.

Person, Group, or Event	Contributions/Results

2. The Civil Rights Movement includes many examples of conflict. For each generalization about conflict listed below, describe a situation that occurred during the Civil Rights Movement.

Conflict arises from differences in people's beliefs, needs, values, or practices.	
Conflict resolution may be violent or nonviolent.	
Conflict may support political, social, or economic change.	

Handout 12.1: Civil Rights Movement Postassessment, continued

3. Congratulations! You have been hired as a historian to write a new book about the Civil Right Movement. You want to be sure to focus on democratic citizenship. Tell about two examples of democratic citizenship you will select to include in your book.

REFERENCES

Ashenfelter, O., Collins, W. J., & Yoon, A. (2005). *Evaluating the role of Brown vs. Board of Education in school equalization, desegregation, and the income of African Americans* (NBER Working Paper No. 11394). Washington, DC: National Bureau of Economic Research. Retrieved from http://www.nber.org/papers/w11394

Ask anything: 10 questions with NAACP President Rev. William Barber. (2008). Retrieved from http://www.wral.com/news/local/story/4142989/

Auditorium, Farmville [Photograph]. (1951). Records Group 21, Records of the District Courts of the United States (1865–1991), NARA's Mid-Atlantic Region (Philadelphia). Retrieved from http://www.archives.gov/education/lessons/davis-case/#documents

Auditorium, Moton [Photograph]. (1951). Records Group 21, Records of the District Courts of the United States (1865–1991), NARA's Mid-Atlantic Region (Philadelphia). Retrieved from http://www.archives.gov/education/lessons/davis-case/#documents

Barton, P. E., & Coley, R. J. (2010). *The Black-White achievement gap: When progress stopped.* Princeton, NJ: Educational Testing Service. Retrieved from http://www.ets.org/Media/Research/pdf/PICBWGAP.pdf

Brown v. Board of Education of Topeka, 347 U.S. 483 (1954).

Dirksen Congressional Center. (n.d.). *Major features of the Civil Rights Act of 1964.* Retrieved from http://www.congresslink.org/print_basics_histmats_civilrights64text.htm#open

Dirksen Congressional Center. (n.d.). *Voting Rights Act of 1965* [Summary]. Retrieved from http://www.congresslink.org/print_basics_histmats_votingrights_contents.htm

Dorothy Davis et al. v. County School Board of Prince Edward County, VA, et al. (103 F. Supp. 337, 1952).

Education Week. (2001). *Quality counts 2001: A better balance.* Retrieved from http://www.edcounts.org/archive/sreports/qc01/

Educational separation in the U.S. prior to Brown map [Map]. (2008). Retrieved from http://commons.wikimedia.org/wiki/File:Educational_separation_in_the_US_prior_to_Brown_Map.svg

Francis, D. R. (n.d.). The effect of Brown v. Board of Education on Blacks' earnings. *NBER Digest.* Retrieved from http://www.nber.org/digest/dec05/w11394.html

Friedan, B. (1963). *The feminine mystique.* New York, NY: W.W. Norton.

Harry Briggs, Jr., et al. v. R. W. Elliott et al. (98 F. Supp. 797, 1951).

Ifill, G. (2004). Brown v. Board of Education 50 years later. *PBS NewsHour.* Retrieved from http://www.pbs.org/newshour/bb/law-jan-june04-brown_5-17/

Liberty Hill colored [Photograph]. (ca. 1950). South Carolina Department of History and Archives. Retrieved from http://americanhistory.si.edu/brown/history/4-five/clarendon-county-2.html

Malcolm X. (1963, November 10). *Message to grassroots* [Speech]. Retrieved from http://teachingamericanhistory.org/library/document/message-to-grassroots/

National Archives. (n.d.). *Federal records pertaining to Brown v. Board of Education of Topeka, Kansas* (1954). Retrieved from http://www.archives.gov/publications/ref-info-papers/112-brown-board-educ/judicial-records.html

National Archives. (n.d.). *Transcript of Brown v. Board of Education* (1954). Retrieved from http://www.ourdocuments.gov/doc.php?flash=true&doc=87&page=transcript

Norris, M. (2004). Parker High: Integration's unfulfilled promise. *National Public Radio.* Retrieved from http://www.npr.org/templates/story/story.php?storyId=1869257

Orfield, G. (2009). *Reviving the goal of an integrated society: A 21st century challenge.* University of California at Los Angeles, The Civil Rights Project. Retrieved from http://civilrightsproject.ucla.edu/research/k-12-education/integration-and-diversity/reviving-the-goal-of-an-integrated-society-a-21st-century-challenge/?searchterm=reviving%20the%20goal

Orfield, G., & Lee, C. (2004). *Brown at 50: King's dream or Plessy's nightmare?* Cambridge, MA: Harvard University, The Civil Rights Project. Retrieved from http://civilrightsproject.ucla.edu/research/k-12-education/integration-and-diversity/brown-at-50-king2019s-dream-or-plessy2019s-nightmare/orfield-brown-50-2004.pdf

Orfield, G., & Frankenburg, E., with Ee, J., & Kuscera, J. (2014). *Brown at 60: Great progress, a long retreat, and an uncertain future.* University of California at Los Angeles, The Civil Rights Project. Retrieved from http://civilrightsproject.ucla.edu/research/k-12-education/integration-and-diversity/brown-at-60-great-progress-a-long-retreat-and-an-uncertain-future

Public statement by eight Alabama clergymen. (1963, April 12). Retrieved from http://www.massresistance.org/docs/gen/09a/mlk_day/statement.html

Records of the Supreme Court of the United States. (1955). *Brown v. Board of Education of Topeka, Implementation Decree; May 31, 1955; Record Group 267.* Washington, DC: National Archives.

Sanchez, C., & Jaffe, I. (2004). *Fifty years after 'Brown v. Board of Education': Patterns of immigration often create schools contrary to ruling.* National Public Radio. Retrieved from http://www.npr.org/templates/story/story.php?storyId=1751945&from=mobile

Southern Poverty Law Center. (2013). Brown v. Board: Where are we now? *Teaching Tolerance, 34*(25). Retrieved from http://www.tolerance.org/magazine/number-25-spring-2004/feature/brown-v-board-where-are-we-now

Spottswood Thomas Bolling et al. v. C. Melvin Sharpe et al. (347 US 497, 1954).

Statement by Alabama clergymen (1963, April 12). Retrieved from http://web.stanford.edu/group/King/frequentdocs/clergy.pdf

Summerton graded [Photograph]. (ca. 1950). South Carolina Department of History and Archives. Retrieved from http://americanhistory.si.edu/brown/history/4-five/clarendon-county-2.html

Teach for America. (2012). *TFA on the record.* Retrieved from http://www.teachforamerica.org/tfa-on-the-record

Tefera, A., Frankenberg, E., Siegel-Hawley, G., & Chirichigno, G. (2011). *Integrating suburban schools: How to benefit from growing diversity and avoid segregation.* Los Angeles, CA: UCLA The Civil Rights Project. Retrieved from http://civilrightsproject.ucla.edu/research/k-12-education/integration-and-diversity/integrating-suburban-schools-how-to-benefit-from-growing-diversity-and-avoid-segregation

Tilly, C. (2004). *Social movements, 1768–2004.* Boulder, CO: Paradigm Publishers.

United States Courts. (n.d.). *Brown v. Board of Education re-enactment.* Retrieved from http://www.uscourts.gov/educational-resources/get-involved/federal-court-activities/brown-board-education-re-enactment.aspx

U.S. Department of Education Office of Postsecondary Education. (2011). *Preparing and credentialing the nation's teachers: The Secretary's eighth report on teacher quality based on data provided for 2008, 2009, and 2010.* Retrieved from http://www2.ed.gov/about/reports/annual/teachprep/2011-title2report.pdf

WhiteHouse.gov. (2014). *Your right to equal pay: Understand the basics.* Retrieved from http://www.whitehouse.gov/issues/equal-pay

Weitekamp, M. A. (2010). *Lovelace's woman in space program.* National Aeronautics and Space Adminstration History Program Office. Retrieved from http://history.nasa.gov/flats.html

Wittstock, L. W., & Salinas, E. J. (n.d.). *A brief history of the American Indian Movement.* Retrieved from http://www.aimovement.org/ggc/history.html

APPENDIX A
CONCEPT DEVELOPMENT STRATEGIES

INDUCTIVE REASONING

One way of guiding students to conceptual development is an adaptation of the work of Hilda Taba. This strategy engages students in inductive reasoning. Students make generalizations only after data are gathered and organized. The data gathering enables students to note the common characteristics of a concept.

STEPS IN THE CONCEPT DEVELOPMENT PROCESS

The steps in the concept development process include:

1. *Generate examples of the concept.* What are some examples of the concept? List them. Try for many examples.
2. *Group similar examples and develop categories.* Put like things together. Put every one of your examples into a category. Label the categories.
3. *Develop nonexamples.* Can you think of something similar that is just different enough that it is a nonexample?
4. *Create generalizations.* Now generate some statements about the concept that are just about always true in every situation.

GRAPHIC ORGANIZER FOR CONCEPT DEVELOPMENT

Ask students to complete the graphic organizer in a small group (see Figure A.1). It is important that thinking go beyond the individual, so that each student's conceptual understanding is modified or reinforced. Completing the organizer alone does not allow for this active thinking.

Direct students to first think of examples of the word and record them in the upper left quadrant. Next, students record what they know to be the characteristics of the chosen concept. These are recorded in the upper right quadrant.

Thinking of nonexamples is difficult for students, but it helps them to understand the difference between this concept and others closely related. For example, for the term *citizen*, a nonexample might be someone living in a country as a visitor. Finally, students form a definition of the concept that they can agree upon. Precision of language is developed here and students come away with a much clearer understanding of the concept.

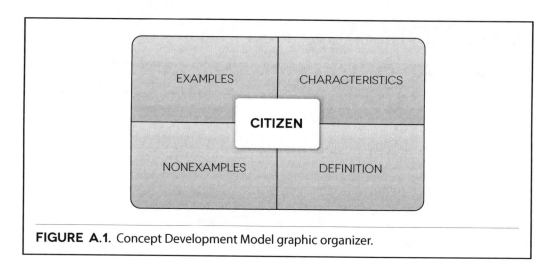

FIGURE A.1. Concept Development Model graphic organizer.

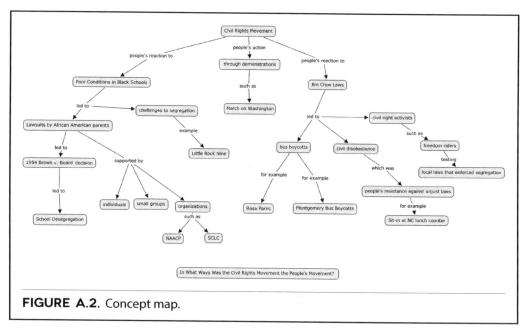

FIGURE A.2. Concept map.

CONCEPT MAPPING

For more expansive concept development, engage students in concept mapping. You may use one of the essential questions as a focus and then ask students to elaborate on that question by mapping their idea. Ask students to place each separate idea in an oval shape and branch ideas with connecting lines. Finally, ask students to write a connecting word on the line to show the relationship from one concept to the other.

Figure A.2 includes an example of a concept map focused on the question, "In what ways was the Civil Rights Movement the People's Movement?" Note that you should select one topic for a concept map. It might be a person, a group, an event, or a question. This becomes the focal point from which students map their ideas. Start with a simple topic for students' initial attempt at concept mapping. Examples of topics for this unit might include:

- ➤ The Birmingham Campaign
- ➤ The Process of School Integration
- ➤ *Brown v. Board of Education*
- ➤ How did the ideas of Dr. Martin Luther King Jr. and Malcolm X differ?

ABOUT THE AUTHORS

Janice Robbins, Ph.D., teaches graduate courses in gifted education at the College of William & Mary. She was formerly Curriculum Chief for the Department of Defense Schools worldwide as well as a district gifted coordinator, principal, and teacher. She recently served as director of a U.S. Department of Education-funded Javits demonstration grant, Project Civis.

Carol Tieso, Ph.D., serves as Associate Dean for Academic Programs and an Associate Professor of Gifted Education at the College of William & Mary. Additionally, she teaches graduate courses in gifted education and research design and recently served as coprincipal investigator on a U.S. Department of Education-funded Javits demonstration grant, Project Civis.

COMMON CORE STATE STANDARDS ALIGNMENT

Grade Level/ Cluster	Common Core State Standards in ELA/Literacy
Grade 6-8 Speaking and Listening	SL.6.1 Engage effectively in a range of collaborative discussions (one-on-one, in groups, and teacher-led) with diverse partners on grade 6 topics, texts, and issues, building on others' ideas and expressing their own clearly.
	SL.6.2 Interpret information presented in diverse media and formats (e.g., visually, quantitatively, orally) and explain how it contributes to a topic, text, or issue under study.
	SL.6.3 Delineate a speaker's argument and specific claims, distinguishing claims that are supported by reasons and evidence from claims that are not.
	SL.6.4 Present claims and findings, sequencing ideas logically and using pertinent descriptions, facts, and details to accentuate main ideas or themes; use appropriate eye contact, adequate volume, and clear pronunciation.
	SL.6.5 Include multimedia components (e.g., graphics, images, music, sound) and visual displays in presentations to clarify information.
Grade 6-8 Literacy in History/ Social Studies	RH.6-8.1 Cite specific textual evidence to support analysis of primary and secondary sources.
	RH.6-8.2 Determine the central ideas or information of a primary or secondary source; provide an accurate summary of the source distinct from prior knowledge or opinions.
	RH.6-8.4 Determine the meaning of words and phrases as they are used in a text, including vocabulary specific to domains related to history/social studies.
	RH.6-8.5 Describe how a text presents information (e.g., sequentially, comparatively, causally).
	RH.6-8.6 Identify aspects of a text that reveal an author's point of view or purpose (e.g., loaded language, inclusion or avoidance of particular facts).
	RH.6-8.7 Integrate visual information (e.g., in charts, graphs, photographs, videos, or maps) with other information in print and digital texts. RH.6-8.8 Distinguish among fact, opinion, and reasoned judgment in a text.
	RH.6-8.9 Analyze the relationship between a primary and secondary source on the same topic.
	RH.6-8.10 By the end of grade 8, read and comprehend history/social studies texts in the grades 6–8 text complexity band independently and proficiently.

Grade Level/ Cluster	Common Core State Standards in ELA/Literacy
Grade 6-8 Writing in History/ Social Studies	WHST.6-8.1 Write arguments focused on discipline-specific content.
	WHST.6-8.2 Write informative/explanatory texts to examine a topic and convey ideas, concepts, and information through the selection, organization, and analysis of relevant content.
	WHST.6-8.3 Write narratives to develop real or imagined experiences or events using effective technique, relevant descriptive details, and well-structured event sequences.
	WHST.6-8.4 Produce clear and coherent writing in which the development, organization, and style are appropriate to task, purpose, and audience.
	WHST.6-8.7 Conduct short research projects to answer a question, drawing on several sources and refocusing the inquiry when appropriate.
	WHST.6-8.8 Gather relevant information from multiple print and digital sources; assess the credibility of each source; and quote or paraphrase the data and conclusions of others while avoiding plagiarism and providing basic bibliographic information for sources.
	WHST.6-8.9 Draw evidence from literary or informational texts to support analysis, reflection, and research.